THE ENLIGHTENED DAD

A Guy's Guide to Surviving the First Years of Fatherhood

by

Andy Geesen
and
Bart Allan

Copyright © 2007 Andy Geesen and Bart Allan
All rights reserved.

ISBN: 1-4196-7583-4
ISBN-13: 978-1419675836
Visit www.booksurge.com to order additional copies.

CONTENTS

FOREWORD 1

CHAPTER 1 Pregnancy: The New Frontier 5

CHAPTER 2 D-Day 17

CHAPTER 3 The Red Zone 25

CHAPTER 4 Health, Safety, and Keeping the Economy Moving 39

CHAPTER 5 Your Tanking Social Life 49

CHAPTER 6 The Diaper Dilemma 55

CHAPTER 7 Havens from the Hellions 69

CHAPTER 8 Your Evolving Vocabulary 79

CHAPTER 9 "The In-Laws are Coming, The In-Laws are Coming!" 95

CHAPTER 10 Clothing Your Toddler: Focus on the Bare Necessities 101

CHAPTER 11 Freedom 109

CHAPTER 12 High (Chair) Fashion 115

CHAPTER 13 Getting Out of Town: The Family "Detention" 119

CHAPTER 14 Birthday Parties in the New Millennium 127

CHAPTER 15	Minivan Mayhem	139
CHAPTER 16	Miscellaneous Rantings and Ravings	149
CHAPTER 17	A Few Closing Thoughts	153

Foreword

> "Before I got married, I had six theories
> about bringing up children.
> Now I have six children and no theories."
>
> **-- John Wilmot**

Each year in the United States, over four million babies are born. Fortunately, most of these infants' mothers are well prepared and eagerly awaiting their arrival. And it's easy to see why. Bookstores, libraries, and newsstands are literally filled with information, testimonials, and advertising geared for and aimed at the pregnant mother. For the well-read mom, pregnancy will likely bring few surprises. Each week of her pregnancy has been broken down and analyzed through a myriad of literature and videos. Additionally, moms seem to have a vast social network that is only too eager to provide an earful of "expert" advice.

In sharp contrast, the soon-to-be-father has very little to guide him. His friends are nearly useless, either because they are still trolling for the right gal at the local pub or because they too are fumbling in the dark, searching for enlightenment. Sure, there are a few books that a guy can buy at the bookstore, but they are either written by some PhD (clinical, boring, and not for "real" men), a woman (if a guy wanted a woman's view on fatherhood, he'd ask his wife), or a celebrity. No offense, guys, but it's difficult to imagine Al Roker, Wayne Gretzky, or Ray Romano groping for baby formula at 4 a.m.

For most men, the wife's pregnancy occurred as a result of yet another negotiation wherein he lost. And even in cases when both the decision to have a baby and the timing of procreation were mutual, the pregnant father has likely remained in a state of quasi-denial. Though he may acknowledge impending fatherhood, he has left most of the "intelligence gathering" to his spouse, opting instead to stay current with the latest rumors involving his favorite sports team as the trade deadline approaches.

The Enlightened Dad serves as the ultimate "guy's guide" to pregnancy and the early stages of fatherhood. The book is a survival manual for the neophyte father entering this challenging period. It is intended for he who wishes to become a good father while maintaining some semblance of dignity and sanity in the process. In order to be a "deer in the headlights," a man needs to first see the light(s)!

And while this book is by no means a technical reference for raising children, it will provide a clearer idea of what to expect once they arrive. The simple fact is that most expectant fathers are ill prepared and under-equipped to handle what's headed their way. The good news: the difficult times of early fatherhood will eventually end. Before too long, a young child will be walking, talking, and potty-trained (all of which generally make things a lot easier for his parents). In fact, even during those tough first years, both Mom and Dad will periodically discover the many incredibly rewarding aspects of parenthood. Where appropriate, and at the stern recommendation of our wives, we have tried to point out some of these "high points" throughout the book. It's not all gloom and doom! (Although some of the ominous aspects of early fatherhood tend to make for better humor!)

So sit back, read, absorb, and, most importantly, enjoy. If nothing else, as you venture out into the new exciting and terrifying world of parenthood, you'll come to realize that your experiences are not unique. Many others before you have experienced your pain and pleasure, and a few have even lived to write about it!

Chapter 1

Pregnancy: The New Frontier

"I don't know why they say 'you have a baby.'
The baby has <u>you</u>."

-- Gallagher

So here you are. Despite being comfortable with a permanent dating relationship, you've been bribed, coerced or threatened into tying the knot. And though your marriage makes things a little different, life moves on pretty smoothly. Yeah, you've had an argument or two, and your wife only likes *some* of your friends. You might have even encountered an incident of marital "bait 'n switch" (for example, your "low-maintenance" girlfriend who loved to cook has suddenly developed a taste for fine jewelry and expensive restaurants). But, all in all, your life has been cruising along. Social opportunities abound, and your relationship has continued to grow.

Suddenly, something new has appeared on the horizon. Through a complicated medical procedure known as "peeing on a stick," your wife has determined that she's pregnant. A trip to the OB/GYN confirms your miracle. The two of you can barely contain your glee!

Well, Rookie, have we got news for you. You've just been called up from the minors. Your life has changed forever, and you don't even know it yet. You will soon experience joy, love, and pride (as well as frustration, pain, and suffering) at levels previously unimaginable. Indeed, some of these emotions will envelop you all at the same time. And the nine-month period that you have just entered is just the beginning! It's a wild ride you're getting on. And unlike Mr. Toad's, you can't get off. Enjoy it! Embrace it! And hold on tight!

In a word, pregnancy is <u>tough</u>. Body aches, fatigue, restlessness, constant sleep deprivation, and irritability will prevail. But just remember, it's tough on your wife, too. You see, much is made of, and even more is written about, the trials and tribulations of the pregnant woman. Entire books have been written on the subject! The fact is it is no walk in the park for the soon-to-be father, either. We have feelings, too!

A brief word of caution here: the explanations, theories, and advice thoughtfully doled out in this chapter should be considered "highly confidential," and should certainly *not* be casually bantered about in any social setting. <u>Don't even think</u> of trying to evoke sympathy for your personal suffering, either from friends, family, or worse yet, your wife. This is a <u>no-win</u> discussion with an array of potentially devastating outcomes. Yes, it sucks that you now have to retrieve the beer and guacamole dip from the fridge yourself. Making your own sandwich is indeed a drag. But you are a fool, f-o-o-l, if you try to challenge the issue. In the end, after an argument that lasts longer than you ever thought possible, you'll be lucky if you *only* wind up begging for forgiveness, rubbing her feet and whimpering, "I'm sorry, honey." Better to just avoid the whole ordeal, strap a mini-cooler of frosties over your shoulder, and

PREGNANCY: THE NEW FRONTIER

take the dog for a long walk. By the way, if you do not yet have a dog, <u>get one</u>. He is likely to be your only friend for the foreseeable future, and certainly the only one to genuinely feel your pain. Importantly, as you'll soon learn, he's also the only shot you have at keeping the floors of your car and home somewhat free of petrified organic matter.

Anyway, the major point of this opening chapter is to warn you of an inevitable phenomenon. Technically speaking, pregnant women tend to get a little wacko. Self-proclaimed experts in the industry – and it *is* an industry (Have you started getting the junk mail yet? The coupons? The "parenting" magazines?) – readily acknowledge this behavior and chalk it up to "fluctuating hormonal levels." Call it what you will, but again, don't argue with her or fight it, just try to accept it and "go with the flow." Think of it as you would if you were caught in a riptide. Don't wear yourself out. Be smart!

Symptoms that pregnant women experience tend to vary from sudden nausea and vomiting to having a very short fuse to losing all grasp of logical thinking (by male standards). To make matters worse, pregnant women (at least those with any brains) generally don't drink alcohol. And because they can't drink, you may get the evil eye when you pop a top.

Believe us, you've seen nothing like what's headed your way. That fun-loving, even-tempered, free-spirited sport who has always appreciated your sharp wit and keen sense of humor will turn into an emotional monster overnight. "Overly sensitive" is an understatement. PMS pales by comparison. Treat her a bit like you would a venomous snake – approach with caution. And remember, for the next several months *everything* is gravely serious. Imagine yourself walking through the middle of a minefield wearing size 25 clown shoes. It's inevitable – you *will* take a beating.

Ironically, your wife's fluctuating hormonal levels may have an upside. Her breasts may grow a size or two, and her sex drive is likely to soar. (It's also likely to crash, and you will never know what will happen and when. Remember our advice about going along for the ride. Take her lead and have fun.) This, of course, is opposite to yours, as you battle internally with questions like, "Isn't this a little weird?" or "Won't this hurt the plumbing?" or "I'll never get that Supreme Court appointment if I do this!" The good news is that sex is safe throughout the entire nine months unless a doctor says otherwise. In fact, there are those "experts" we've interviewed who claim that good sex helped to "jump-start" delivery! ("Was it good for you dear?" "Ohh, yes. Take me to the hospital.") Again, rather than relying on our experts, you may want to consult someone who actually knows what he's talking about.

During your wife's pregnancy, the closest thing to childbirth training either of you is likely to get is in a "Lamaze" class (this is one of many new terms that is likely to creep into your vocabulary). Taking a Lamaze course is highly recommended by the industry because it does provide some useful and practical information and it increases their revenues. A Lamaze class is useful in that it gives you some specific information about what is happening inside your spouse's body and what to expect when delivery occurs. The problem, though, is that you are required to sit through eight hours of class in order to get about twenty minutes of valuable information. It's a bit like traffic school. If you should be lucky enough to stumble across an enterprising opportunist in the hallway shadows who is selling a Cliff's Notes version of Lamaze, <u>buy it</u>. If not, here's the basic summary:

1. Delivery is painful.
2. Your wife needs support.
3. Numbers 1 and 2 don't matter anyway, because she's getting an *epidural*.[1]

Lamaze classes can be taken either privately or in a group and are often offered through local community colleges or hospitals. These classes tend to be taught by earth-mother types who wear sandals and espouse all things natural. They may or may not shave. Though it's often useful to learn from other couples' questions and experiences, smaller classes generally tend to be more valuable. This is especially true if you're anything like George, who simultaneously managed to

---

[1] In semi-medical terms, an epidural is an injection into the outer layer of the spine. Practically speaking, it's a big needle that goes into your wife's back when she's in labor. By the time it's administered, she will likely be experiencing considerable pain as the contractions grow more intense and occur in greater frequency. Incidentally, if jealousy issues exist in your marriage, they are likely to surface at this point. The anesthesiologist is that fellow you've seen all day pacing the halls of the obstetrics ward like the grim reaper – this guy could be a 4' tall ogre with missing teeth and a bad comb-over…It doesn't matter. When you finally cave in and let him "do his thing," this guy becomes your wife's Knight in Shining Armor. She will whimper in happiness as all feeling (read: agonizing pain) below her waist quickly fades away. You haven't seen adoring eyes like hers since your first date. But hang in there, champ. The epidural doesn't last forever. Before long, she'll be abusing him, too.

embarrass himself while creating a lasting memory among his Lamaze classmates.

> Please note: In most of the testimonials throughout this book, names have been changed in order to protect the fathers (including the authors) from further humiliation and/or spousal retaliation.

A few months into Nancy's pregnancy, she starts yacking about registering for Lamaze. At first, I argued that she should go alone, or with some of her other pregnant friends. Mistake. Disgusted (and quite verbally so), she explained that this is not done, and that I needed to play a part in the preparation of the birth of <u>our</u> child. Not normally good with either blood or doctors, I figured the closest I'd ever get to a delivery room was the nearest bar that allowed cigar smoking. But after three weeks of hearing about Lamaze every night, I reluctantly gave in and promised to join her in the class.

The next thing I know, I'm being dragged, like a cat to water, down to some woman's house for the first "session." Sensing my resistance, Nancy teases me at dinner with a tidbit of information which she had gathered while enrolling – that one of the couples is not a "he and she" but rather "two she's." I quickly became a little more eager to finish my meal and dash off to class. This might not be so bad after all...

As it turned out, there were seven couples in our class, plus the instructor, for a total of fifteen people. The "gay" couple that had lured me in was a false alarm – just a girlfriend "sitting in" for the husband, who was either traveling (for the entire six weeks over which the class ran), smarter than me, or both.

The first class focused on relaxation techniques. I hung in there for a while, but the quiet meditation period did me in. The pizza and beer I downed at dinner made for a volatile concoction, and the resulting movements of gas within my stomach became quite audible. My attempts to cough and fake sneeze were unsuccessful at masking the noises, which grew progressively louder. Tom and Sheila, a couple who sat just to our left and who eventually became good friends of ours, said later that their sides ached from trying to hold back their laughter. Toward the end of that very same class, after my stomach had returned to "normal" and I was finally able to relax, another problem emerged. I got <u>so</u> relaxed that I managed to fall asleep for a few moments, and my first snore apparently shook *up the entire class. I was forever branded. And though the class was held just two miles from our home, that drive home was the longest of my life. Among her other rantings, my wife made me acutely aware of the embarrassment and humiliation which I had "single-handedly" bestowed on every member of our family, both alive and yet unborn. Before each subsequent class, Nancy made me eat a salad and limited me to only one beer. Fortunately, after an exhaustive search, I found a local barbeque joint that served up a cold one in a frosty 30 oz. "fishbowl" mug. Lemons to Lemonade. From then on, Lamaze class was a piece of cake.*

For those of you with spouses who are needing or planning a caesarian section ("C-section" in the industry), congratulations! You've just been handed a "Get Out of Jail Free" card. You can skip Lamaze, because your spouse will be sedated and timed breathing is irrelevant. But beware. Any perceived advantages of a C-section will be quickly wiped out after childbirth, as the recovery period from this surgery can be lengthy (Read: You will be the housekeeper, cook, and family chauffer for at least several weeks).

One event during your wife's pregnancy that you definitely won't want to miss will be the "ultrasound." At about the twenty-week mark, she will schedule an appointment with a specialist who, through the miracle of modern technology, will actually enable you to view, with unbelievable clarity, the fetus in the womb. *Make time to join your wife for the ultrasound.* It's truly an amazing opportunity to get a "sneak peak" at your child.

Basically, the process of performing an ultrasound goes something like this: after rubbing a petroleum-based jelly over the surface of your wife's ever-expanding stomach, the doctor will run a small sonic probe over the area. On a video monitor, you and your wife will be treated to an amazing real-time look at your yet-unborn child. It's a very emotional moment – likely to draw tears from even the most hardened macho-types. (You might want to just "happen" to have some stashed Kleenex for those nasty allergies you've been fighting.) And as good as these images are today, ultrasound technology is rapidly improving, with 3-D imaging and continually higher resolutions. Since most facilities have video recording equipment, be sure to take a blank tape or DVD with you.

Worth noting are just a few other observations from those of us who have battled before you in the trenches. First, during their pregnancy, moms can get ultra-hungry, and without any build-up or warning. Instantly, no one is in a good mood. Try to convince her to carry a Power Bar or a bag of saltines in her purse, and encourage her to snack at the slightest hint of hunger. In fact, take it to the next level, and insure yourself against a run-in with the two-legged piranha. Place little "food stations" everywhere – throughout the house, in the garage, even in the car. Make sure she's never more than a step or two away from a sack of munchies.

Secondly, with the fetus growing by the day, your wife's bladder will get compressed to the size of a grape. In the third "trimester" (medical jargon for the final three months of pregnancy), she'll be headed to the bathroom every 30 minutes. To the extent that you enjoy sleeping, you'll want to plan your escape routes – to the guest bedroom, couch, garage, etc. Typically, you'll want to "execute" your exit as soon as it appears that she's actually asleep. And be sure and practice your escape regularly – each of these routes will be used time and again when your kids start climbing into your bed in a few years.

Third, beware the dreaded morning sickness. Essentially, this affliction makes women feel like they have a constant hangover (or so we're told). Despite the name, it can occur any time of day. If you see your wife reeling about the house looking green and clutching her stomach, she likely has morning sickness – or she just tried your cooking. Typically, this passes after the first trimester, just in time for the "Giant Belly" phase.

Finally, a fate that has befallen a few of our unlucky friends is that sometime during the second half of pregnancy, the wife is put on "bed rest." This term is a death sentence to any man who values his free time. It simply vanishes. Any waking moment not spent toiling at work is spent waiting on the wife and preparing for childbirth, basically doing the job of two. If this happens to you, *bring in the reinforcements* – <u>immediately</u>. Think what you may of your mother-in-law, but trust us, she is far more capable of gaining control of the situation than you. And if you already have a toddler or two running around, this is a no-brainer. *You need help… and fast.*

Ignore this sage advice and you'll pay a heavy price: a pigsty of a house, delinquent bills, malnutrition. No need to get yourself in an early hole, because it doesn't get any easier when your wife and child return home and you enter the "Red Zone," the dreaded period outlined in Chapter 3.

Chapter 2

D-Day

> "Giving birth is like taking your lower lip
> and forcing it over your head."
> **-- Carol Burnett**

Get ready. Delivery Day ("D-Day") is fast approaching. There you'll be, behind the desk in your cubicle, minding your own business and deciding which greasy spoon deserves your lunch patronage, when the phone will ring…

"Can you come home now? I think I'm going into labor!" Assuming this is not the third time you've gotten a similar call and/or you're convinced it's not another false alarm, gather your belongings, log off of eBay, and head for the homestead. If her water has broken[2], you may want to quicken your pace. But regardless, <u>don't panic</u>. It's not like the scene in that Monty Python movie where the obese guy is begging for just "one more mint," after which he suddenly explodes. Usually, you will have plenty of lead time. And your wife won't explode. In fact, it is not uncommon for a mother to start dilating weeks before she actually goes into labor. For a first-time mom, it may be <u>difficult to discern</u> the cramps she's been experiencing over the

---

[2] The water breaking is the event that occurs when the sack containing the amniotic fluid (which has protected the fetus during the pregnancy) ruptures, and the fluid rapidly exits the mother's body. In Lamaze class, this is said to be just a small amount of liquid, maybe a "cupful." We beg to differ. In fact, when their wives' water broke and they were nearby, several of our esteemed interviewees reported initially thinking a plumbing joint had burst.

past couple of months from the pains of contractions. So to the best of your ability, try to be patient and understanding. It may be a little painful, but this is one situation where you want to err on the side of caution. And be sure to enjoy that ride home. It will likely be the last for at least a couple of decades where you won't be worrying about something fatherly.

Upon arriving at the hospital, and assuming that you've done your pre-delivery homework, your wife will probably just need to sign in, and the two of you will be escorted to a Labor and Delivery room. You will then need to settle in and endure some of the longest hours of your life. Just like an airplane pilot might describe his job as countless hours of boredom interrupted by moments of sheer terror, so will you describe your pre-delivery hospital experience. There will be long hours spent waiting for contractions to get closer together, with a "target" dilation of ten centimeters[3]. At times, you are sure to get discouraged and impatient, thinking it'll take forever to get to 10 centimeters. But hang in there. Things happen a lot quicker when she reaches 7 centimeters than they do at 3 centimeters.

A word of caution on a subject not covered in most Lamaze classes. During this time, not many kind words will come your way from the wife. And while harassing and berating you and your side of the family, she will likely order you around like

---

[3] Regardless of your wife's size, shape, or astrological sign, 10 cm seems to represent the proverbial checkered flag. This is the point at which the cork is ready to leave the bottle. Why this is the magic number is well beyond our scope of research.

some kind of gopher. Our advice: swallow your pride. This doesn't last forever. It's probably just the inevitable result of a bad mix of drugs and hormones. Again, there is no upside to arguing, or in trying to defend yourself and anyone with your last name. Take your licks, try to make her comfortable, and move on. If you really want to be proactive, bring along a few of her favorite CD's or, better yet, create a mellow playlist for her iPod. Calming music tends to soothe everybody's nerves.

On a positive note, there will definitely be some intimate moments between the two of you during this period – times when, despite your excitement and anxiety, you are able to take in the magnitude and enormity of this life-altering experience. The only possible comparison to this intense anticipation might be Christmas Day when you were a child – when you just couldn't wait for the big moment to arrive. Remember: The most important part of your being there is to lend support and encouragement as her partner during this shared experience.

When the good stuff finally starts to happen, you will need to hunker down. Seriously, the birth of your child is a miracle you do not want to miss. The real action starts when your wife starts pushing in sync with her contractions, usually with the doctor and several nurses present. After some time, the baby will start crowning.[4] At that point, things get very exciting. But rather than butcher the facts, we'll leave your education

---

[4] Crowning assumes that the baby exits the mother "head first." In some cases, if the baby did not turn in the womb, it is said to be "breech," and a cesarean section may be required.

with regard to the particulars to your childbirth or Lamaze class. To describe all the good stuff now would be to deny you your money's worth in the classroom.

A few key points need to be made here, however.

First, after the birth of your new baby, don't get too excited about calling the relatives right away. Take a little while to "chill out," to celebrate and enjoy the event with mother and child. Don't let your excitement get the better of you. For example, it's definitely not cool to phone your mother- and father-in-law just moments after the birth, while the doctor is sewing up your wife's episiotomy.[5] For one thing, you're probably in the way of the doctors and nurses, who still have a lot of work to do. Also, the in-laws will surely want to speak to their daughter, who is likely to be a little out of commission. Better to let her settle down and "regroup" before attempting to recount her experiences.

Second, though you may be tempted, DO NOT take photos you will live to regret. Remember, you're going to be emotionally caught up in the moment. Unless you've gotten the wife's <u>prior written</u> permission, it's usually not a brilliant idea to send those pictures of her privates down to be processed and evaluated by the local, pimply-faced teenager that works in the one-hour photo lab or some remote on-line processing center. Take our advice and save your shots (at least the still photos) for the gooey baby wipe-off and baby-with-mother scenes.

---

5 Consult your wife.

Finally, know this: in nearly all cases, the childbirth process is a lot less "gory" than the father expects. Speak to most men who have witnessed the event, and they will tell you that the birth of their child is something they would not miss for anything in the world. And as a reward for your efforts, the doc will usually let you snip the umbilical cord (if you desire to do so). So don't be afraid to be with your wife as she gives birth to your baby. It's a very special time for both of you, and your support will be much needed and appreciated.

We stress this last point because, in conducting our "research," we were told time and again that the experience of childbirth was much more joyful and enjoyable than the soon-to-be-fathers had imagined. As a group, most of us "modern" guys have been over-exposed to the thinking and philosophies of our fathers, many of whom simply dropped off their wives at the hospital and then waited with their other six kids for the phone call.

The true story below is typical of those "horrid" accounts of childbirth to which many of us have been exposed. Importantly, this pathetic tale is meant *solely for your enjoyment and amusement*. It is *not* meant to indicate what actually might occur in the delivery room, and there is absolutely no reason for this to happen to you!

> *Several years back, one of my co-workers, John, and his wife, Kathy, had a lovely baby girl whom they named Ashley. Not long after returning*

to work the week following Ashley's birth, John exclaimed that I <u>must</u> see the videotape he had shot of the delivery.

I was horrified. Ashley's birth, I reasoned, was a very private, blessed event. Any accounts or pictures taken were very personal, meant to be seen only by John and Kathy and chosen family members. But John persisted. He promised me that I not only wouldn't see anything improper or gory, but added that the video was "hilarious."

A hilarious childbirth. He had piqued my interest. So off to the conference room we went, during our lunch break, with three or four other curious Neanderthals. Lights off, VCR on. I'm covering one eye, dreading my squeamishness when the blood starts going everywhere...

The video starts normally enough. John, not known either for his sensitivity or camera work, is panning around the hospital room in the opening scene, proudly noting that the baby's timing will allow him to catch both Final Four match ups on that particular Saturday. What a lucky guy. //CUT// Kathy is visibly uncomfortable as contractions start to kick in. She is upset with John, who is doing his best to comfort her while fumbling with the video camera and catching some of the pre-game show. //CUT// Kathy is writhing in pain and screaming obscenities at John, who seems unaware that the camera is still recording. //CUT// The Grim Reaper (a.k.a. the anesthesiologist) has arrived and has inserted the epidural. Kathy seems to be settling down. At least the screaming has stopped. John can be heard muttering in the background how the Reaper's presence has thus nullified all time and money invested in Lamaze class. Kathy doesn't seem to care. //CUT// John and the Reaper are perched at the foot of Kathy's bed, rooting for opposite teams in the nightcap. Kathy looks irritated, but her eyes don't seem to be focusing. //CUT// The doctor and two nurses are counting loudly, "...eight, nine, ten, PUSH!" Kathy grimaces for a few seconds, then begins yelling the obscenities again. Something about a jackass, a bowling ball, and it's 'your fault,' "...eight, nine, ten, PUSH!" John seems to be losing his steady hand. As the baby starts to emerge from behind the sheet which is covering Kathy's lower body, the camera sways left, then right, then upwards. There is much audible commotion, but the only thing being filmed is the ceiling. In the background, the doctor can be heard requesting smelling salts for *"the husband on the floor." John has not only passed out cold but has immortalized himself by recording the faux pas. //CUT// Kathy and Ashley leaving the hospital. Video camera is now being operated by someone else. //CUT// Out of the shadows emerges John, sheepishly sporting his new head bandage. //CUT// The happy couple, with baby Ashley, recovering at home. Listening to an account of the ordeal, John's father can be seen in the background, glaring at his son, gently shaking his head and rubbing his temples. //CUT// FADE TO BLACK.*

Chapter 3

The Red Zone

"Child rearing myth #1: Labour ends when the baby is born."
-- Unknown

The period immediately following the birth of your little angel(s) will surely lure you into a false sense of security. Your wife is happy, your parents and the in-laws proud, gifts abound, and everyone wants to take care of the newborn baby, who sleeps silently most of the time. Don't be fooled. The baby will eventually wake up, the presents and congratulatory phone calls will cease, and the relatives vanish with their photos once the initial thrill is gone. You will suddenly feel like you're standing in a sand storm with your pants around your ankles. Welcome to the "Red Zone."

Before further explanation, it is worth mentioning that the number of relatives at the hospital, the number of friends that call, and the amount of presents that arrive are all *inversely* related to the number of children you already have. In other words, expect a big crowd (read: lots of help) for the arrival of your first child. By the third delivery, your parents will have forgotten that your wife was even pregnant. Family and friends will assume that you know what you're doing and that you've got the routine down. Big mistake.

Soon after the crowd clears out and you begin to realize the hell that you're in for, a number of curious "objects" will start popping up around the house. It is during this period that you will get to see some of your "pre-delivery" purchases or shower gifts in action for the first time. Though there is literally no limit to the accessories you might run across, we have outlined below several key gadgets and contraptions which will be especially scary to you if you have not been forewarned about them and their uses.

<u>The Breast Pump</u>
Due to a variety of reasons, you may run into the need to extract "liquid gold" (a.k.a. breast milk) for use at a later time or date. For this purpose, the modern breast pump fits the bill. And speaking of bills, you and your wife will, at some point, likely have some basic discussion regarding the buy/lease decision of this apparently benign mechanical device. (Hint: Ask yourself the following three questions: What is the pump's "residual" value? How likely is some misguided sap to pay that amount? And, perhaps most importantly, what will it be worth to you to have the thing out of the house once you're done with it? No, it doesn't store well with the wedding dress.) Unless you plan on emulating the Brady Bunch and economies of scale are expected to kick in, the lease program is probably the better option. Regardless of all this sound logic, of course, your wife will buy her own pump.

Your first run-in with the breast pump is an event you will not forget. Consider the experience of Mark, age 39:

THE RED ZONE

There I was, driving home after my first full week back at work. Everyone at the office was very excited for me and still eager to see the pictures of my son, Justin, born two weeks before. As I entered my neighborhood, though tired, I was generally in a good, upbeat mood.

My first sign that things were amiss occurred as I pulled my car into the garage and turned off the engine. Almost immediately, I noticed a faint, muffled buzzing sound, which seemed to be coming from inside the house. A faulty electrical wire, maybe?

Not quite. As I opened the door, the sight I gazed upon was one I'll never forget so long as my lungs are drawing air on this planet. There, before my naked and unprepared eyes, sat my wife Lori with this contraption of tubes and cups rigged up to her. Obviously in discomfort, she seemed to be wrestling with this mechanical monster, which appeared to be drawing milk at the rate of two drops per hour. To be perfectly honest, I didn't know whether to laugh, cry, or flee in horror. One thing's for sure, though. I will never, ever, think of my wife's breasts in quite the same way again. Though I eventually became accustomed to the buzz (as opposed to the sight) of the breast pump, this little gadget engrained in me a theory which I hold strongly even today, years after my initial "run-in": if procreation and the development of infants were dependent solely upon males, the human race would be extinct within two to three generations.

For the months that followed, I became amazed at the number of frozen milk bags that filled our freezer. I had to develop quick hands in order to remove my ice cream without having thirty little frozen white rocks tumble out and smash my bare feet. Each night, included in my prayers was a plea to God that my refrigerator not break down. And though I never acted upon my fears, I often thought a back-up generator would allow me to sleep more soundly.

The Diaper Genie

Oh, if only this thing would grant you three wishes. This is another gadget you will get to know well, and if you know where to invest your money, you'll have several of these throughout the house (so as to minimize the distance you have to carry a wet and smelly diaper). On the downside, by using the Diaper Genie you actually have *three* chances to wretch and/or gag. Your first opportunity will arrive when you stick a saturated diaper into this container. A second shot to heave will present itself as you unload the twisted bag inside (which, when filled, looks like a chain of overgrown sausages and smells like death warmed over) and haul the whole mess to the trashcan. One hint here: Try to haul the full bag out just *before* the trash man arrives. Leaving this thing in the garbage bin for more than a day or so allows for fermentation, an especially disgusting phenomenon in July and August—thereby affording you a third and final chance to toss.

All joking aside, though, you *need* a Diaper Genie.

The Baby Monitor

There is no doubt that the first Baby Monitor was invented and designed by a woman. Its basic purpose is to allow the paranoid mom to listen to her baby from afar. For reasons too extensive to cover in one book, you will curse the jackass who gave you this dreaded "gift" at the baby shower for years to come. It is not enough that you must listen to your kid's screaming from down the hall. No, you must have this hideous noise amplified and echoed thanks to this wonderful little gadget. And if you need to wander outside the house for any reason, no worries. The damn thing works on batteries too. The Baby Monitor is living proof of technology's dark side. It is one of the rare child-related devices that should be destroyed rather than passed on. An M-80 in the battery compartment does the job nicely.

One subtle bit of upside with regard to the Baby Monitor: it may, from time to time, allow you to tune in to your neighbor's arguments (or other activities), as the frequencies on your respective Monitors get crossed up. Of course, this can be a good or bad thing, depending on who your neighbors are and how lively their arguments, etc. can get.

All joking aside, you *do not need* a Baby Monitor.

<u>Other Trends to be Aware of</u>
Besides stumbling upon mysterious new gadgets such as those described above, you will notice several other key happenings around your house during the Red Zone period. For some of the dilemmas you will run across, we are eager to offer preventative measures and/or helpful solutions. As you might guess, however, some of the phenomena continue to baffle even us.

<u>Your Role as Head of the Household</u>
As a young child, you probably held your father in high esteem; in your eyes, he was a hard working, dignified man, worthy of the respect given to him by his wife and children. Around the house, his word was Gospel. As you now fill what was your father's role, you will likely come to realize that either times have changed or your childhood views of fatherhood were way off. To paraphrase the late Rodney Dangerfield, "You will get no respect."

Through conversations with friends, you will be assured that your lowly status on the home front is anything but unique. Apparently, it is quite common for the arrival of the first child to cause a sudden and dramatic shift in a new mother's priorities.

Whereas, during courtship and (in most cases) following marriage, the man and his happiness were the woman's top priority, the bewildered new father must now fend for himself, attracting all the attention and affection of a kitchen rug. It is indeed a cold shock when you find out that the only one who now seems to relate to you is your faithful dog, who, to his own disbelief, now gets even *less* attention.

This "call to reality" is well documented by Peter, 38, now father of three:

> *During Karen's first pregnancy, I often found myself working long hours at the office. First off, I knew that I would need to take some time off after Matthew's birth. But also, my home was becoming a hostile environment for all the obvious reasons. Anyway, through my hard work, I earned several successive promotions, eventually leading to a position of Senior Vice President with management responsibilities for several large projects and over fifty people.*
>
> *What I soon discovered was that my life was becoming something of a paradox. Whereas at work I had become a relatively high level executive whose leadership and advice were sought after, at home I was viewed as a bumbling idiot. My views and opinions, once revered, quickly became unwanted and*

irrelevant. After our child was born, I was trusted neither to hold nor feed him for fear I would drop him or cause some sort of choking. And, of course, I was always being told that I was "too loud."

<u>Odds 'n Ends</u>

A number of additional Red Zone phenomena that you are likely to encounter are worth mentioning. Again, it's not like you're going to avoid these pitfalls altogether. But as long as you're going to get punched, you might as well get your hands up.

- As a neophyte father, you'll need to become acquainted with the concept of the "Museum Home." Basically, according to the Museum Home Theory, which will be adopted and employed by many a new mother, your home can look like an atomic bomb just went off when you walk in after work, but God forbid if so much as a painting is crooked when guests, relatives, or friends come to visit. While this phenomenon may have existed prior to your having children, its frequency, as well as the amount of effort you'll need to expend in order to attain Museum Home status, will soar once kids arrive. With kids and all their related crap, preparation for museum status usually takes no less than four hours and is primarily your responsibility. When complimented by visitors, your wife will attempt to convince them that your home looks like this all the time.

- With fatherhood comes a whole new array of trick questions from the wife. Be especially wary of this trend in the Red Zone. For example, an old interrogation (with no known answer) might have been something like, "How do I look?" or "How do you think this outfit fits me?" Once kids arrive, questions can get even tougher. A new trick question might be, "I know you'll be with clients tonight and it's good for your business, but *if you had a choice*, you'd rather stay here at home with the children and me than play poker with those guys, *wouldn't you*?" For God's sake, just take the 5th. And pace yourself at the table.

- Beware of "mass thinking and behavior" on the part of your wife and her friends. For example, watch what happens when one of the mothers from the kids' play group insists that, according to some "reliable" reference or report, the Peg Perego stroller is the SAFEST (a key term to become especially wary of). Hint: if it is publicly traded, buy stock in Peg Perego immediately. The rest of the mothers will flock like sheep to buy the product, so as to not be left behind or outdone. Without fail, the "safest" highchair, car seat, stroller, swing, or medicine will be twice the price as the second safest item. A "no-brainer," you will be told by your better half as you throw down your credit card, hoping at this point just to get the hell out of Babies 'R Us.

- Existing happily in the Red Zone will require that you make one of the most critical investment purchases of your life – a box of earplugs. Used properly, earplugs can play an enormous role in improving your quality of life. You'll be happier, more productive, you'll sleep deeper and for longer periods, you'll get along better with your co-workers, and your wife's friends will become much more tolerable. Leave 'em in all day – you will be glad you did!

- Even with the help of a quality pair of earplugs, the experience of a good night's sleep will quickly become a distant memory. It is therefore a good idea to keep a couch in your office and to drive a car with a roomy back seat. And always be sure to keep a pillow in your trunk.

- Just before going to sleep each night, make it a habit to clear the path between your side of the bed and the guest bedroom (or couch or whatever your retreat). Many will be the mornings when you wake up in your "back up" lair with no recollection of having gone there. You will want to avoid a nasty sleepwalking injury.

THE RED ZONE

- Finally, while enduring life in the Red Zone, be very careful about wandering too far away from home with your child. To illustrate, consider the pathetic experience of Stan:

My biggest [Red Zone] faux pas occurred on a beautiful autumn Sunday afternoon. After watching a little pigskin on the TV, I decided that I would go out and get some exercise while, at the same time, knocking down some quality bonding time with my 3 month old daughter, Lilly. I bundled the little cutie in a warm outfit and tucked her into one of those three-wheeled jogging strollers. Off we went, parading down the sidewalk. Cars literally pulled off the road, and neighbors rushed out of their homes to see Lilly, whom I was only too proud to show off. It was the perfect scene – loving father, cooing infant, an Indian summer afternoon in Southern California.

Suddenly, our idyllic existence turned into a nightmare. Without warning, while smiling and giggling at an admiring couple from down the road, Lilly had a loud and violent blow-out. I, of course, had forgotten to bring a spare diaper on our little trek. Crying turned to screaming, and a brisk walk turned into an all-out sprint. The same neighbors who, just minutes before, came out to admire the two of us now watched in horror as we dashed homeward. All of the neatly packed contents were now flying out of the stroller, and I couldn't have cared less. My only priority was to get that child home and into her mother's arms.

Clearly, Stan's biggest mistake was in venturing too far from home. Our advice to fathers who find themselves in a similar "stir-crazy" situation is to wander out in "concentric circles" away from the home base. If one outing goes OK, take a slightly bigger "loop" the next time. But whatever you do, don't get overconfident, and always be ready to return home on a moment's notice. The punishments for avoiding these unwritten rules can be severe, a fact to which almost any new father can personally attest.

Chapter 4

Health, Safety, and Keeping the Economy Moving

> "A woman knows all about her children. She knows about dentist appointments, soccer games, romances, best friends, location of friends' houses, favorite foods, secret fears and hopes and dreams. A man is vaguely aware of some short people living in the house."
> **-- Unknown**

Childproofing Your World

At some point during your wife's first pregnancy (usually after about six to seven months), the topic of "childproofing" will rear its ugly head. Maybe the subject will first come up in childbirth class. Maybe the conversation will occur at the home of another new parent. Worse yet, you'll be assaulted with this topic while in bed—late at night, of course. There you will be, trying to drift off to a utopia of bachelorhood and responsibility-free existence (a.k.a. college). Your wife will suddenly put down the *Parents* magazine she's been memorizing, yank the drool-soaked copy of *Sports Illustrated* off your blissful mug, and exclaim, "Honey, you know we should start baby-proofing the house..." (The funny part of this sentence is the liberal use of the word "we." If you can actually envision your wife breaking out the cordless drill and a Phillips screwdriver, you shouldn't be reading this book.)

When first confronted with this "safety" issue during your wife's pregnancy, your mission is clear, and you must act quickly and confidently. *Change the subject* or simply put it off, if this is at all possible. Derail or distract her. Yell "fire!" Do anything to avoid getting sucked into this premature conversation. The fact is that this discussion has very little reason to occur for at least another year, if at all. Save yourself the wasted brainpower of designing the foolproof set-up to safeguard your little treasure, for all the reasons outlined below.

First, to a large degree, childproofing is a fallacy. As self-proclaimed experts, we subscribe to the notion that, like in the case of a thief trying to enter a home, safety devices will only manage to slow the guy down. With most "modern" childproofing devices, however, you get the added bonus that your kid may injure himself in the process.

Consider the testimonial of John, age 27 and father of two toddlers:

> *My wife and I knew we needed to put a safety gate at the top of our staircase. After staring at the box in the corner of the master bedroom for two months, I finally got my act together one Saturday and, with a little sweat and profanity, managed to install the thing. Though the gate stayed in place and worked well in preventing premature learning of the skill of tumbling down stairs, it did have one major design*

HEALTH, SAFETY, AND KEEPING THE ECONOMY MOVING

> *flaw. The metal latch on our gate is exactly 28" off the ground. As luck would have it, our 18 month old child's eyes are also right about 28" up. Sure enough, as little Trevor passed through the gate, it "rebounded" off the wall, and the latch caught him in the forehead, just missing his eye. Blood curdling screams slowly faded into prolonged crying. Luckily, the only damage was a good-sized bruise. In retrospect, there was little I or any other attentive adult could have done to prevent this incident from occurring. Trevor had been injured by a device that had been intended to protect him...So much for "childproofing"...*

Another reason to forego, or at least delay, serious childproofing efforts is our contention that most children manage to stay out of real trouble until they start walking. This usually occurs anywhere between months 9-15. Ironically, soon after you child is able to walk, you will rue the day when she took her first steps. Greater mobility spells greater curiosity, resulting in quicker trouble. In basic terms, you will lose your ability to simply open a drawer in order to retrieve that Tylenol you so badly need. And we won't even discuss the consequences of neglecting to move the shaving cream to higher ground.

Childproofing methods and devices come in a wide variety of forms. The most common are the plastic latches for drawers and cabinets. Don't be fooled into thinking that you can just stumble into Home Depot (or worse, get dragged to the local Babies 'R Us) and pick up a slew of these overpriced plastic gizmos. You can, but you'll likely soon be returning for different ones. Do a little homework. Take a look at each cabinet and drawer in your house and observe where and how a safety latch might be attached. There is no "universal" solution. Also, try to figure out which cabinets and drawers really *need* to be protected. If you do it yourself, mounting these things is neither fun nor quick. Should you choose to hire out and have them installed, it ain't cheap. And, believe it or not, there will be times when you'll *welcome* the concept of your kid preoccupying himself by rearranging the contents of the Tupperware drawer. At least this way you can catch an occasional 4th quarter or the beloved catnap, so long as the little one stays away from the Ginsu knives!

Another popular form of childproofing are the strips of padding that conveniently adhere to the edges and corners of tabletops and fireplaces. The intent, of course, is to cushion the blow when Junior looses his balance and smacks his head on the furniture. In theory, the stuff should work pretty well, though it makes your family room look more like Romper Room. The problem with the padding, though, is really two-fold. First, as soon as you manage to install the stuff, Junior will find a new, more dangerous place to go bang his head. Installing protective padding is like trying to find the end of a rainbow; you never quite solve the problem, and ultimately, the only thing *not* padded turns out to be the dog, who takes a liking to chewing the stuff. Secondly, sooner or later, you'll find

HEALTH, SAFETY, AND KEEPING THE ECONOMY MOVING

yourself trying to wrestle a four-foot section of the stuff out of the toilet while it overflows. Sheer misery. Here's a valuable tip: When you're ready to "pad" your furniture, cruise down to local hardware store and pick up some foam pipe insulation. Cut it to fit. And that's it! – Quick, simple, and a fraction of the cost of a similar product at any overpriced children's store.

A few more comments on our favorite kid-proofing device – those protective "fences." The bad news on these gadgets is that they can be dangerous – not only for kids (as discussed previously), but for parents too! These tricky little contraptions tend to "disappear" at night, catching you in the crotch and sending you into your silk ficus collection. When this does inevitably occur (either to you, your wife, or your vision impaired mother-in-law), you not only get the distinct pleasure of re-installing the fence, but also of repairing and repainting the three foot sections of dry wall that were torn off in the process.

On the positive side, here's what you have to keep in mind as you ponder how you're going to make your 24" fence fit a 28" opening (the hardware in the box is intended for the "ideal" scenario, which of course does not exist in your house): fences *do* indeed manage to keep kids out of, or away from, a particular area. Or viewed another way, they are very useful in keeping kids *in* a certain space. Don't necessarily think of a fence solely as a device to keep your children *away* from the stairs; think of it as a tool to keep them *in* their rooms. You might actually consider a fence for the hall closet, effectively creating a mini jail cell for your little monster. Now *there's* a new twist on the over-used "time-out" concept! Incidentally, your ideas about childproofing devices, and the use of fences in particular, will likely deviate vastly from your wife's. Women seem to take a very *preventative* approach to protecting their children; men, on the other hand, tend to want their kids to actually *learn* from their mistakes, thereby minimizing the chance of repeated occurrences. For instance, moms are generally big fans of installing gates at the top of staircases. Most fathers would argue (unsuccessfully, as usual) that nets at the bottom of the stairs might be more effective. A detailed analysis of these differing views on child safety, as well as discipline, will be saved for a sequel in order to prolong our marriages...

One final note on childproofing: Once you have done all we've suggested – latched the cabinets, protected the drawers, padded any sharp edges, installed protective fences – and you finally think you're "done," think again. Now, you need to find all potentially breakable items, sharp or semi-sharp gadgets, anything that could fit in a child's mouth, and put all this stuff in a box. Go find a place in the garage that's unlikely to be disturbed for the next ten years (hint: put it next to your wife's bridal dress that you've unknowingly committed to store for eternity – that's another box that won't be touched for a long time). Finally, dress your kid appropriately. Outfit him in such a way as to minimize the chances of an accident. Fit him with thick wool mittens, so he loses the effectiveness of his fingers. Stick him in an inflatable sumo wrestler costume, one that will reduce or negate the impact of any collision. And lastly, get

HEALTH, SAFETY, AND KEEPING THE ECONOMY MOVING

him to wear a snug fitting full-faced motorcycle helmet. We promise, this solution will cost less, take less time to install, work better, and provide you a little entertainment along the way.

On a serious note, we strongly advise that you keep a close eye on young toddlers. It is astounding how quickly they move, even when crawling. And when it comes to finding trouble or danger, Murphy's Law applies. Without fail, it's the one time the gate is unlocked that they'll go through it, and the one unlatched cabinet in the house that they will happen to find. Always keep poisons, cleansers, and medicines in high places, and if you have a pool or other body of water on your property, take any and all precautions available. Give yourself and your kids a large margin for error, and hope that you'll never need it.

<ins>The Pediatrician's Office: Your New Second Home</ins>
No chapter on child health and safety would ever be complete without a brief discussion about your child's pediatrician and, more importantly, your new role as his annuity. Talk about job security. Simply put, toddlers are sick a lot. And even when they're perfectly healthy, most mothers feel inadequate if they don't at least "check in" with the pediatrician on a regular (and frequent) basis.

At some level, possibly subliminal, any pediatrician has to laugh when a paranoid mother makes her eighth trip to his office in less than a week. Try this, just as an experiment: when your second child is about 6 months old, take your wife's car out of the garage, point it in the general direction of the kids' doctor, hit the gas, and let go of the steering wheel. Chances are, her minivan will track the worn grooves in the pavement between your home and Doc's parking lot. On the occasions when you're stuck taking the kids in, be sure to ask their doctor if he offers a "frequent visitor" program. Or maybe a deal where every tenth visit is free, like the car wash or the local donut joint. He'll probably just laugh—or glare at you like you're some kind of alien.

There is really no excuse for any intelligent pediatrician to be anything short of an expert in whatever hobby he chooses to pursue. If it's sailing he prefers, Doc should be a master yachtsman. If it's golf he fancies, he ought to carry a single digit handicap and look like a million bucks doing it. These guys earn enough dough to afford the latest equipment and clothing, and with just a few paranoid mothers as clients, they can "cluster" their appointments, resulting in plenty of free time.

And then there's the doc's sidekick, the pharmacist. In the "ideal" arrangement, the pharmacist is to the pediatrician what Bonnie was to Clyde, Hardy to Laurel, Larry to Moe. Acting on illegible instructions from his accomplice, the pharmacist will line your shelves with an array of bottles, tubes, jars, and syringes, all the while whacking away at the ol' deductible. The whole miserable scam will come to light one cold, dark morning when your wife asks you to go and fetch the kid's medicine. If you're lucky enough to find that needle in the haystack, you get the pleasure of lining up the (misaligned) arrows, a challenging task in the bright light of day, let alone the wee hours of the morning.

This is where the humorous differences between mom's and dad's measuring techniques become very obvious. Dad usually takes a guess at how much medicine looks about right, similar to the collegiate practice of adding butter and milk to the macaroni and cheese. Mom, on the other hand, will spend 15 minutes at 4 a.m. measuring each molecule of pink goo with Swiss-like accuracy.

With regard to the application of your child's medicine, avoid cups at all cost. You will wind up having to bribe and coerce the kid into taking his medicine, often a long and arduous process. Rather, get yourself a small collection of syringes, CO_2 powered if possible. Maybe by the time this book hits the shelves, some Einstein will have developed a way to convert your paintball gun into a medicine delivery device. Your kid may choke and gag a bit, but the medicine will go down quickly and relatively easily. You and your child will be back to sleep, sawing logs, in no time!

Practically speaking, dealing with a sick child can be somewhat more complex. To begin with, when a real crisis hits, the medicine never seems to work quickly enough. But often, the hardest part is in recognizing that something is actually wrong in the first place. Sure, when you realize that the spaghetti coming out of your child's nose is actually a stream of snot, you might reasonably conclude that he has some sort of sinus-related problem. But other ailments, such as a digestive problem or the ever-dreaded ear infection, can sneak up on you, often not making themselves known until the middle of the night. You'll think your baby is just having a bad night, and depriving you of some much needed rest. You might even find yourself getting angry. But have a little patience. No, have *a lot* of patience. An infant or toddler can't talk, and crying is his only way to communicate and express his misery and frustration. Never hesitate to call the pediatrician at 2 a.m.; it won't be the first or last middle-of-the-night call that doctor gets.

Chapter 5

Your Tanking Social Life

"Having a child is surely the most beautifully irrational act that two people in love can commit."

-- Bill Cosby

Fatherhood is to a man's social life what the iceberg was to the *Titanic*. Not that, by reading this chapter, your fate will differ from that of the captain of the "unsinkable" ship. Any remnant of your social life is "going down" for reasons soon to be outlined.

With the certainty of your forthcoming demise into obscurity, it is our humble opinion that an official "going away" party is in order. Because that's exactly what you'll be doing – *going away*. Believe us, that spontaneous part of your personality – the drive to make a surprise "drop in" on a friend or to tip a pint into the wee hours – is going into hibernation for a few years. So why not throw a formal "send-off" to say good-bye?

OK, so you're not buying it. You are different. You and your wife have your act together, your roles are well-defined, and your priorities are in order. You will *not* turn out like your cousin Elroy, whose idea of a weekend outing is a trip with his wife and three kids to the local Costco, Wal-Mart, or Target.

Well, we'll see. Granted, this is not an easy concept to embrace. And it may not happen to every man. But for the majority of us, the time demands on a new father are unbelievable. And the social arena, like that newly hired middle manager, will likely feel the axe first. Right or wrong, fair or not.

At first, changes will be subtle. After the initial "shock" (see Red Zone), you'll start venturing out again – to a party or two, maybe a nearby restaurant, or to friends' homes. "I'm bucking the odds!" you'll proudly claim, convinced that you've nimbly dodged the demise that consumed poor Elroy. But then, at some point, a stark realization will occur. Clinging to a conversation with an old friend at a party, margarita in one hand and a fussy and/or disinterested toddler in the other, it will hit you that *this is not worth the effort.* Neither is the embarrassment and humiliation you will feel in any restaurant as you subtly try to kick the smattering of food beneath your kid's high chair under an adjacent table.

Before you know it, the most current movies you will see are already on their second release in the video store. You will become an expert on the Friday night TV lineup. Restaurants in your neighborhood will open, become very popular, and go out of business before you get a chance to sample their fare. The only couples who will come for dinner or to visit are those you met in Lamaze class and whose lives are obviously in similar disarray. Your social life is *accelerating* downhill.

At this point, you may be saying to yourself, "It's OK. I'll just assemble an army of babysitters." Son, you are in for a rude awakening. Before recruiting your "army," try some simple arithmetic: start with the entire population of the world; eliminate immediately those folks who live outside of a ten mile radius of your home; further nix those individuals who are simply not interested in babysitting; then narrow the field to include just those who you think will respond to your wife's benign ad in the local paper (of course, basic stated requirements include a paramedic's knowledge of CPR, a post-graduate degree, twenty years of "related" experience and no less than thirty solid references); further eliminate those who then fail to survive your wife's grueling interview or your mother-in-law's fierce cross-examination. Chances are, just a few hearty souls remain in the candidate pool for your "army." Finally, eliminate from contention any remaining individual who either doesn't call back after the interview or fails to return after their first stint with your kids. In the end of your analysis, you will reach the inevitable conclusion that there is not one person living on the planet who is both qualified and willing to stay alone with your kids.

And as if this harsh slap of reality is not brutal enough, you will further discover that your existing pool of friends is dwindling as well. Before long, it will become apparent to both you and your wife that your friends *without* children, no matter how tight your friendship with them, just won't *get it*. They don't *get* ten-minute attention spans. They don't *get* crushed Cheerios in their carpet or cheddar fish crackers in their car. They don't *get* the fact that a nine month old can't keep himself busy. They can't relate to conversation without occasional profanity. And they sure won't understand how their nine o'clock (p.m.) phone call could possibly wake you up! (When this latter event does finally occur, by the way, you can know that *you've arrived*. Social demise is complete.)

On a closely related subject, we have made an interesting observation and have developed our own corresponding theory. To illustrate, next time you're on a commercial airplane and a toddler or infant is screaming bloody murder, look around and take note of the range of reactions exhibited by the surrounding adults. In all probability, there will likely be several people drawn to the child in an effort to help or sooth her discomfort. Conversely, there will be those who scramble for an open seat (as far away from the noise as possible) or subtly stuff their ears with Kleenex while staring bug-eyed straight ahead. Our theory is that, generally speaking, a person's patience level or propensity to help this screaming child is directly proportional to the number of kids they have (or have had) at home. You will be much more empathetic to the child's parents after you've endured a few of these miserable flights as a parent yourself. So much for theories…

Getting back to our main subject, it will be important for you, as a new parent, to come to grips with the fact that those without kids may be that way for a reason. Now that you've got 'em and they don't, you've become oil to their water, and never the two shall mix. Remember, no one will ever tell you that they don't like kids. Indeed, they themselves may genuinely believe that they like these little novelties. Yet the fact remains that, unless they're yours, kids tend to wear on adults after an hour or so. And this will undoubtedly lead you and your wife to spend many a Friday or Saturday night at home getting to bed early because your children don't yet see the value of "sleeping in."

During this "anti-social" period, it's important to keep in mind that this too will eventually end. In the meantime, try to make the best of it – learn to appreciate some of the simpler things in life. A good pizza ordered in, a fine bottle of wine, and a classic movie can go a long way in soothing your (and your wife's) frazzled nerves. Interestingly, when your social life finally does begin to re-emerge, many of your new friends will be parents of your child's little pals (obviously, a direct result of your common life experiences).

Thus, after some of your old friendships have waned, new ones will start to develop. But, whereas in your previous life a conversation might begin "Do you think her rack is all natural?", it will now be more like "So have you heard that K-Mart is having a sale on Supremes…?" or "Have you *seen* that new Honda Odyssey?"

Chapter 6

The Diaper Dilemma

"Diaper backward spells repaid. Think about it."
-- **Marshall McLuhan**

Incoming!...

> "...there she was, standing in her familiar spot, grimacing, not breathing – the dead giveaways of a toddler pooping (a.k.a. going #2). To make matters worse, my wife had run off to do some errands. This was my "shift." No problem, I thought. This was not the first diaper I had changed. So I lay her down to start unsnapping her pants when I realize that my right hand and right shirt sleeve were wet. And they were halfway up her back! The alarm sounds off in my head – 'Monster Dump! Get her up quick!...' I lift my little girl up, turn her around, and my worst fears are instantly confirmed..."

To all you freshly ordained, wet-behind-the-ears fathers, in order to fully appreciate the severity of the crisis described above, you'll need to recall your former role as a college prankster. Before the onset and dominance of audio compact discs, there were LP's (record albums) and their accompanying cardboard jackets. If you're old enough to recall, one of the ways to really annoy a friend who had wisely locked his dorm room door was to fill up a record jacket with shaving cream, quietly slide the open end under the door, then stomp on the remaining portion of the record jacket. The resultant force flings the shaving cream all over the inside of the room, covering your "friend" and his half-dressed co-ed companion (who subsequently flees in horror). Even if you've never experienced such stupidity, you hopefully get the picture.

We use this analogy because the diaper story above employs the same basic laws of physics: take a substance of relatively low viscosity, force it through a small opening, and the stuff travels far...and fast. In the opening passage, by laying the kid down, the diaper's contents were forced violently outward, exploding up the back of her shirt and all the way to her hairline. No advice is likely to prevent such a mishap; it's just inevitable bad luck. Pray to the God of Firmness.

There are a few critical things you will need to learn in order to handle the Diaper Dilemma. More accurately stated, there are certain specific ways to know when you need to vacate the premises to avoid having to change a dirty diaper and general rules to follow when escape becomes impossible.

First, as a normal, blue-blooded American male, your primary goal should be to change as few diapers as possible, especially of the #2 variety. This is one instance where the spousal "teamwork" thing gets thrown out the window. To this end, it will become critical that you begin to recognize the early warning signs of impending dumpage. You will need

THE DIAPER DILEMMA

to become an expert in "tuning in" to the key indicators, as outlined below, *before* your wife.

Typical tip-offs to an impending stooge:

- Child goes to a certain "spot" in the house or may even attempt to hide
- Child stops moving, stands erect or with knees slightly bent, fists clenched
- Child stops babbling/talking, possibly grunts
- He/she will have a funny, strained look on face
- Eyes may water slightly

Again, early recognition of these telltale signs will be all-important. If you can spot these phenomena before your wife, you've bought yourself valuable seconds of escape. If possible, get yourself immersed in a "messy" project – finger painting or changing the car's oil – so that your wife will have no choice but to solo the diaper change. At a bare minimum, get her between you and the soiled diaper, then argue "law of proximity."

One of the classic cartoons we've seen serves to illustrate this point quite well. In the cartoon, two hikers encounter a large bear in the forest. As they start to run from the bear, one of the hikers stops to change into running shoes. "Those shoes are not going to help you outrun the bear," the one hiker says to the other. "I don't have to outrun the bear," the other hiker sagely replies, "I just have to outrun you!"

Imagine you and your wife as the hikers. Your kid is the bear. Get those shoes on!

Inevitably, however, there will be instances where, for whatever reason, you get caught adjacent to your kid when it's discovered that Junior has soiled his drawers. In such cases, quickness on your part will be key. Whenever possible, whisk the kid outside – your chances of minimizing "collateral damage" (to your clothes, his siblings, the carpet, family pets, etc.) will soar, and the stench seems to dissipate more rapidly outdoors.

When hauling your little stinky bundle out to the backyard, try to exit the house through a sliding door. Your hands will be busy, and a slider is easier to open with your hip. In the case of the occasional "extreme blow-out," when clothes become "histo" (this is what an insurance agent would term a "total loss" – believe us, you'll know it when you see it), you may want to cut the child's clothes off him rather than slipping them over his head. Either way, your best friend will become a garden hose with good water pressure. Finally, try to avoid telling your wife what you're doing until it's over. Women always want to "save" clothes and for some reason hate to hear that their children are being "hosed down."

<u>The Disposable Diaper</u>
As a new member of the Fraternal Brotherhood of Neophyte Fathers (FBNF), you are about to encounter and utilize one of the most amazing inventions of the twentieth century – the disposable diaper. Seriously, it ranks right up there with

the light bulb and the telephone. The fact that American high school students are not required to study the life of its anonymous inventor is yet another example of our failing educational system.

You know the exotic animals that you see on those weird nature shows that can devour prey three times bigger than they are? Well, think of disposable diapers in the same way. They are literally capable of handling the periodic severe flooding problems of small towns lining the Mississippi River. Just throw a few Huggies Supremes at the encroaching floodwaters and watch the parched ground start cracking. The guy who figures out how to make paper towels out of the same revolutionary material will be an instant millionaire. In the name of water conservation, never, ever, let your child enter a swimming pool while wearing a disposable diaper; once the kid exits the pool, so does the water!

Sooner or later, your wife will ask you to catch your child and "check his diaper," which basically means that she wants you to make a determination as to whether or not the kid needs a new one. The most common type of field examination is the "smell test," a quick sniff of the child's buttocks region. If you remain conscious and can still see straight, you will be required to determine if the limit of urine absorption has been exceeded. Obviously, this is somewhat subjective, and your perceived limit is likely to be greater than your wife's. A rule of thumb here: after removal of clothing, if the Huggies sags down and touches the floor, you can generally write that diaper off as being "maxed out."

And herein lies the beauty of the modern disposable diaper. Once it has "done its job," you can get rid of it! No soaking, no wringing, no washing, drying, or sticking yourself with safety pins. Just clear the area, remove the thing, (try not to gag), roll it up, and shove it into the Diaper Genie. No fuss, no mess!

But now for the downside, however slight and irrelevant. As great as these things are, they are not free. In general, they'll set you back about $.25-$.50 each, depending on the size (smaller diapers are less expensive). This doesn't sound like much until you consider the fact that small kids use up diapers faster than Hugh Hefner burns through Viagra. Infants require about fifteen diapers per day, a figure that tapers down to about 6-8/day just before potty training, a blessed event that occurs after about 24-36 months. Even after they're potty trained, however, you will continue to use a "pull-up" version for a while until you build the courage to let the kid go diaperless overnight. All told, we estimate total diaper use at somewhere between 8000 and 9000 units, resulting in a diaper expense of over $3,000 per child! Importantly, this figure does *not* include expenses for wipes, Diaper Genies, new clothes, carpet replacement, etc. And remember, until the tax code is changed, these are *after-tax* dollars!

At this point, we know what you're thinking. Forget it. Contrary to logical thinking, it really doesn't pay to delay changing a diaper. The smell does not go away, and "economies of scale" play no role here. Your kid will never crap twice in the same diaper, no matter how long you wait. It's like watching water come to a boil. Without fail, he will either wait until he's naked, or three seconds after you've wrestled him into a new, fresh diaper. It's almost as if kids get corked up when they've already got some action going in their current diaper. Our advice: just go ahead and change your kid's diaper when you suspect things have gone awry. You'll save yourself the embarrassment of having someone else discover the stench and also reduce the chances of diaper rash setting in.

Potty Training
Getting your child potty trained is a bit like getting him to walk – it's a much-anticipated milestone that, once it arrives, turns out to be a mixed bag.

First, you will likely encounter more than a few "false starts." Even after your child is able to understand what you're trying to bribe him to do, chances are he will have an accident or two, especially while sleeping. A stern word of warning here: whatever you do, don't try "pull-ups" until you are absolutely convinced there is no chance of dumpage. If a kid blasts in a pair of these absorbent underwear, you'll have to drag the package the length of their legs to get it off – an unenviable task best avoided if at all possible. (In editing our manuscript, our wives informed us – just prior to publishing – that the sides of pull-up diapers actually rip for easy removal. Nice to know now.)

With regard to potty training, kids seem to learn best by observing their peers. Accordingly, if you have three children, your middle child will probably take less time to get the "potty gig" down than your first child did, and your third will learn even faster. In theory, your tenth kid should never need a diaper. So try to rent an older brother or sister if none is available in your home, or enroll your child in school where they can observe older kids. It's not a fetish at this young of an age, but rather one of the better learning tools you will find.

As usual, our interviews and "research" turned up a solid testimonial on this subject. But as has too frequently been the case, our buddy Mark's story serves more as a lesson in what *not* to do while potty training your child:

> *In the courtyard just outside our home, we have a small outdoor spa that our son, Jake, loves to splash around in. The problem was that the warm water caused him to have to pee every five minutes. At first, I was just glad he didn't assume that he could go in the spa. And since running in and out of the house would irritate his mother, I taught him the male survival skill of peeing into the bushes. Not only did this solve the "wet trail to the bathroom" problem, but the kid seemed to enjoy helping the plants grow taller.*

Unfortunately, Jake then decided to take this general concept to the next level. One day, while I was talking to the next-door neighbor through the wrought iron fence which separates our yards, Jake suddenly decides to drop his drawers and relieve himself on the rose bush directly between us. Acting surprised about how Jake might have gotten such an idea, I actually got a kick out of this first "mishap." My face turned a bit redder a week later, when I had the cable installer out and we were examining where to install the wire. Again, Jake had to go, and did so – unannounced – just a few feet from the cable guy's boots. "Ha, Ha, kids these days…"

The problem reached a climax just a couple days later, when my wife was picking Jake up from his pre-school. As she was buckling him into his car seat, his teacher came running into the parking lot and begged for a moment of her time. "I'm sorry to have to bring this up," she began, "but could you please have a talk with Jake about his going #1? Today, while playing with the other kids in the play area, he suddenly pulled down his pants and peed in the sand. The other boys, as well as one girl, thought this was really cool and were attempting to do the same before we managed to stop them."

> *After receiving a quick third degree from my wife, the two of us attempted to explain to our son that peeing outside was for emergencies only. We thought we had gotten the message through until the teacher again approached my wife several weeks later. This time, little Jake wanted some water to make a better sand castle (an apparent emergency in his mind). Since the teachers forbid the kids from filling up the buckets from the water fountain, Jake took matters into his own hands (so to speak), tried to hide behind a bush, and peed into his bucket. He was busily engaged in mixing the contents of the bucket with a pile of sand when the horrified teachers removed him from the play yard.*

The moral of this tale: Be careful when teaching boys about the joys of peeing in the great outdoors.

Miscellaneous

A few final notes with regard to diapers:

1. Whatever you do, always carry a stocked diaper bag when you leave home with the kids. This is especially true when you "solo" with them to any kind of a "social event." Save yourself the embarrassment of having to leave early by <u>always</u> carrying *at least* two extra

THE DIAPER DILEMMA

diapers per kid along with a healthy stack of wipes. And contrary to what your wife may have told you, a diaper bag doesn't have to have a floral or Disney-theme print. There are plenty of manufacturers whose diaper bags are made to look like normal backpacks.

2. When your wife strolls into the house with her jumbo bags of diapers, grab a big black Magic Marker and make notes on the packages. You see, different diaper manufacturers have different "size numbers," different ways from telling front from back, and varying "thicknesses," or absorption capabilities. And, unbelievably, none of them write any of this on the diapers themselves! So before your wife sticks a bag of Huggies under the bathroom counter, we suggest that you jot something like "Olivia, overnight, flowers-front." This coding will save you an incredible amount of hassle when fumbling for the night diaper in low-light and/or semi-conscious conditions, and the embarrassment of having to explain why both of Livvie's legs are protruding from the left leg-hole of one of her older sister's diapers.

3. Putting diapers on kids is something of an art. It requires practice, finesse, and, most importantly, patience. If you try to force it, it's like solving a moving jigsaw puzzle or wrestling an oiled pig. If the kid is in a good mood, try to keep it that way – and move fast. If they're feisty or cranky, just put in the

earplugs, hunker down, and give it your best shot. And good luck.

Keep these pearls of wisdom in mind in order to avoid more pain than necessary:

Preparation
- Have a least 2-3 wipes already pulled and separated from the stack before you open the diaper.
- Have the new, fresh diaper open and ready to go. The last thing you'll want to do is to have to release your squirming kid from your firm grasp so you can separate the Velcro straps from their packaged position (no normal male we've spoken to has ever claimed to have done this with just one hand). Let him go and your kid will travel a long distance in this short time.

Execution
- *Always lay them on their backs* (repeat this phrase several times). The bonus points earned by occasionally changing the kid standing up are not worth the effort or the risk.
- When removing the diaper, always take pants and socks totally off. Crap is attracted to cotton like iron shavings to a magnet. Again, play it safe.

- After a diaper has been removed, move it a distance from the child that is twice that which you think their arm or leg can possibly reach.
- Having a roll of duct tape by your side is not a bad idea when changing a diaper. If, while putting on the new diaper, you manage to yank off one of the Velcro straps (this can be done very easily), a small piece of duct tape will do the trick. After having read the diaper cost analysis above, you surely know where this tip is headed.

Chapter 7

Havens from the Hellions

"When my kids become wild and unruly, I use a nice safe playpen. When they're finished, I climb out."
-- Erma Bombeck

We all love our wives. We adore our kids. Most of us have even matured to the point that we can tolerate the in-laws (albeit for certain agreed-upon limited time periods). But with all that said, there are still times when we simply need a break. From the wife. From the children. The baby monitor. The chaos. A best-selling book analogized this phenomenon to man's primordial need to "retreat to his cave."

Well, Thor, it's time for you to get a little creative. Yeah, you can ditch the gang by dashing off to work, extending that business trip, even by faking a sickness. But this stuff is bush league, and the purpose of this book is to make you a smarter, savvier father—to get you thinking outside the box, so to speak.

To this end, we have outlined seven "tried and true" methods of temporarily distancing one's self from the kids while gaining a little freedom and sanity in the process. Several of the methods described below will require practice. Others will come more naturally. Some may work better than others in your particular household. Several can be used simultaneously or in combination. Again, use your head. Be creative. And good luck!

1. Catch a Catnap

Just as ducks have developed webbed feet and polar bears have thick fur, so it is that, over the ages, fathers have developed and refined the skill of napping. It's simply a necessary defense mechanism. Call it *Paternal Darwinism.*

And in case you have yet to realize it, that eight to ten hour slumber of years past is history. The ability to "check out" on a moment's notice – previously known to be mastered only by your grandfather and the neighborhood drunk – is a skill you'll need to develop if you hope to avoid mundane chores and maintain any sense of happiness and self-dignity. What "getting a date" means to a boy in his teens, "getting laid" to a guy in his twenties, "catching a nap" is to the thirty-something father. With young children, you need to be able to snooze for short, interrupted periods in virtually any environment. And if your little ones are on the hyperactive or aggressive side, you may want to wear protective gear.

Equally important is the art of "fake napping." What decent, loving wife would make her "sleeping" husband change a soiled diaper? The fake nap requires practice but, when perfected, can be very effective in catching the last few minutes of a ball game. For starters, close your eyes, breathe deeply and consistently, with an occasional random snort or "mini-snore." A little drool out of the corner of your mouth won't hurt either.

2. Join a Gym

Rather than further boring you with third person advice, we'll let Philip, father of two boys, ages 2 and 4, describe his valuable discovery:

> *One rainy Sunday morning, my wife Katie hauled me down to the gym for a "tour." A gym membership was something she had been trying to talk me into for months, but I had balked because I knew it was a sure way to blow $80 each month on something we'd seldom use.*
>
> *The sales gal was rattling on about the quality of the equipment and their "special" low enrollment fee when something caught my eye. Off in the corner was a big, padded room with all kinds of kids' play equipment, separated from the gym by a big, thick, soundproof window. Eureka!*
>
> *Sensing my enthusiasm, the sales gal quickly changed gears. She explained that what I was looking at was the club's brand new "childcare facility," now available to all members. Adding icing to the cake, she further explained that for a mere $2 per child per hour, a trained and certified childcare specialist would supervise my kids. The only caveat to the whole deal is*

that, while your children are being supervised, you <u>must</u> stay at the gym.

Before the salesperson could wrap up her pitch, I went after the bait – hook, line, and sinker. The gym equipment could have been plastic for all I cared. I wrote that check as quickly and as neatly as I could – hoping all the while that the woman wouldn't "discover" an error with regard to the child care rates, or worse, that I would wake up and the "facility" was just a dream. After nearly a year as a member at this gym, I can happily report that my membership has been just that – a dream. Among other things, it has helped me develop the skill of "multi-tasking." I can actually get some personal time while simultaneously giving my wife a much-needed break from the kids. And every once in a while, I actually work out!

3. Strip a Piece of Furniture

Note: This escape trick works only if your wife has a problem with children playing around highly toxic, caustic, and flammable material. From recent observations of the evening news, we do not assume this to be a "given."

If you really need regular breaks from domestic chaos, furniture stripping and restoration are hobbies you may want to consider. The basic algorithm is simple. First, get your wife interested in scouring garage sales for solid wood dressers, chairs, tables, etc. that need a little TLC.[6] This shouldn't be too difficult, since most women love to bargain hunt, and especially in the rare instances when their husbands actually *approve* of it. Second, stockpile the furniture in a garage or nearby storage area. It is critical that you have fast, easy access to your "work." Then, when all hell breaks out on the home front (or alternatively, when your team has a big game and you don't want your enjoyment of the radio broadcast to be interrupted), break out the rubber gloves, SOS pads, rags, and the nastiest paint and varnish remover you can find. Trust us – the kids will disappear. And the term "stripper" will take on a whole new meaning.

What caring mother would ever risk her beloved child's future IQ by allowing him to get near this stuff? Once again, the only one who will hang with you is the dog, who probably isn't too intelligent to begin with and, more importantly, doesn't scream or cry.

4. "Fix" the Car

This nifty little trick is a bit like stripping and refinishing a child's dresser; if you play your cards right, it's a definite win-win. You'll get what you're after – a little free time – and your wife will be happy, too.

---

[6] If your wife actually likes the furniture, or it's a children's piece, you're <u>really</u> ahead of the game!

First, you need to "discover" a problem with her car. It doesn't even have to be a real problem. Disconnect a spark plug wire if you need to, or let the air out of her left front tire (a very dangerous condition, you will lovingly point out, especially when transporting children). Then spend the next few hours at the "mechanic's garage" or at the "dealer," "repairing" the problem. You will wind up redeeming yourself, once again proving yourself to be the caring husband that your wife married. For your part, you've bought yourself some peace and quiet, and she's sure to appreciate your love and concern.

5. Assume Your Rightful Position on the Throne

Think back to your childhood. What better natural defense mechanism does a man have than to lock himself in a bathroom, sit down on the toilet, and contemplate his existence? Most seasoned fathers are masters of this skill. When they "head for the head," their kids avoid them like the plague. Better to go to Mom for help putting on the shoes! Though only marginally creative, this "escape" method has gradually evolved with each new generation of fathers. It is a skill that typically develops with age; grandfathers are great at it!

A few keys to successfully repelling the wife and kids whilst doing one's "business": first, find the smallest restroom in the house (the guest "powder room" will usually do), disconnect the fan, and take in some good reading material. During your "reign," be sure and occasionally shift your position on the seat. By failing to do so, blood circulation to your lower extremities can get cut off. Getting up with your legs "asleep" can be very awkward, and a misstep can result in a mess we won't even discuss. Second, modify your diet so as to maximize your gas output at certain desired times during the day or evening. Finally, when things get really bad on the domestic front and extreme measures are called for, consider taking a "fake dump." Like the fake nap, this practice is useful in providing a few minutes of peace and quiet to the exhausted father. Just don't overuse this method of escape, or it will surely lose its effectiveness. And be sure to lock the door! Your kids will *really* think you've lost it if they discover you on the can, reading, with your pants on.

6. Go Play Golf

If the thought of joining a golf or country club ever crossed your mind, now may be the time. Think what you will about snobbery, elitism, etc, but most golf clubs are tailored for weary warriors trying to escape battles on the (home)front.

You see, the guys who run a country club on a day-to-day basis – the starter, the marshals, even the staff toiling in the grill – they GET IT. They know your pain, and a good part of their job is to "protect" you. If you think you're the first man in history who sneaks in 18 while avoiding the family, think again. When your wife calls the club looking for you, the guy on the other end of the line knows the routine and how to handle her (scathing) inquiry. She's more likely to get quick, accurate information on your whereabouts from a government agency.

A word of caution is in good order here. When evaluating golf clubs, avoid those that emphasize "family entertainment." Remember, your goal is to *escape* the family, not attract them. A swimming pool, for example, is a definite no-no. Who wants to listen to a bunch of screaming rug rats while trying to line up a putt? Worse yet, a swimming pool (or other similar family "gathering spot") will provide the curious wife with a vantage point from which she can determine not only *if* you're playing golf but, often worse, *with whom* you are playing!

So join a golf club, maintain a friendly relationship with the starter and marshals, and you will be "well-insulated." By hitting the links, you will buy yourself four-plus hours of peace, quiet, and serenity. One final helpful hint though: before returning home and especially if it's a weekday, it's a good idea to put your suit or "work clothes" back on. It will minimize arguing. Also, check for grass and sand in your hair before entering the house.

7. Buy or Rent an Extra House

At first glance, this tactic may seem absurd. Hear us out. What would you be willing to pay for a secret "retreat" – a throwback hangout with a fully stocked refrigerator, the requisite poker table, a big screen TV with a remote that is a) locatable and b) works? Out of your league, you say? Not if you and a few of your buddies who are in similar predicaments can pool your resources. Get a group of guys together – the circle of saps in your Lamaze class is a good start – and get each to ante up for his own piece of "father's paradise," replete with gardener and a (young Swedish) "housekeeper." No chores, no nagging, no crying, no diapers, no Barney. Sell it to your cronies as a "single asset REIT" with fringe benefits. It's the best investment you, and they, will ever make – appreciation *plus* yield!

One final note on ditching the kids: once you've gone through all the trouble of establishing subtle and creative ways to temporarily distance yourself from familial chaos, an interesting change will begin to occur. After some period, you'll actually *miss* your kids! You may even have to dream up a reason or two why you had to return home so soon. This is just yet another twisted paradox that is part of becoming a good father.

Chapter 8

Your Evolving Vocabulary

"Small children almost never misquote. In fact, they usually repeat word for word what you shouldn't have said."
-- Etienne Marchal

One of the many benefits of having toddlers around is that you are likely to find your vocabulary quickly expanding. Not only are you exposed to a plethora of new words and expressions (not all in the Queen's English) that require that you assume the role of interpreter, but many common terms will take on entirely new meanings.

Listed below and on the following pages, in no particular order, is a sampling of words and phrases which will probably either be new to you or will take on new meaning as you muddle your way through your first years of fatherhood.

<u>Word or Expression:</u> **SLEEP**
Old Meaning:
>An uninterrupted period, usually no less than eight hours, which generally begins and ends *when you choose*. Upon awakening, you feel refreshed, energized, and ready to attack the day (or night).

New Meaning:
>Sleep quickly replaces beer consumption as the most coveted activity in your life. A good snooze is about

as common as a bona fide UFO sighting. What little rest you get will be for very short periods and will often be interrupted by your newest family member, who possesses entirely different ideas about "sleep requirements." In the morning, as you plod off to work, you will be exhausted, frazzled, and unable to hold a coherent thought. In short, you will feel like you've been run over by a truck. Your worst hangover will pale in comparison. And, best of all, you can count on this cycle repeating itself the next night.

Word or Expression: **SLEEP IN**
Old Meaning:
To lie in bed until noon.
New Meaning:
On its own, this expression will have no meaning, as this concept will cease to exist. The term "sleep in" will simply be two words preceding where you will be crashing. "I'm going to *sleep in* the guest bedroom tonight…" or "Enough. I need to *sleep in* the garage tomorrow night."

Word or Expression: **ONESIE**
Old Meaning:
A "onesie" was a great gal to know in college. Basically, it would take you only one date to get where you wanted to go, thus the term "onesie." Context: *I can't wait 'til Saturday night! I'm taking*

YOUR EVOLVING VOCABULARY

> *that Delta Omega, Julie Jones, out for dinner. I hear she's a onesie.*

New Meaning:
> A one-piece outfit for infants and toddlers. This mass of cotton and snaps is bound to confound, as you try to match up snaps on your writhing child while attempting (futilely) to keep his arms and hands out of the dirty diaper you just removed.

Word or Expression: **PLAY DATE**

Old Meaning:
> In those bachelor days of yore, a "play date" was something you enjoyed with a "onesie." (See *Old Meaning* above.)

New Meaning:
> The modern "play date" illustrates just how much things have changed in a generation. As your child begins to emerge from the infant and toddler stages, this term will slowly creep into your vocabulary. Not long ago, a good part of any child's entertainment (and exercise) was provided through time spent with other kids in the neighborhood – playing in the street, someone's backyard, etc. In many areas today, such random gatherings of children are very rare, if not unheard of. The modern "play date" is a pre-planned get-together of two or more children, usually arranged days (or weeks) in advance by their mothers.

Word or Expression: **BAH-BAH**
Old Meaning:
> The sound a sheep makes.

New Meaning:
> A baby bottle.

Word or Expression: **LAMAZE**
Old Meaning:
> A 24-hour road race and endurance test which takes place annually on the streets of a small town in France.

New Meaning:
> The class you'll be taking soon. *Lamaze* is actually the name of the Frenchman who discovered the psychoprophylactic method of childbirth while working with Russian women in the '50's. The term "Lamaze" now generally refers to a class wherein pregnant couples learn about childbirth, watch some Discovery Channel-type videos, practice meditation and loud breathing, and stick clothespins on their ear lobes.
>
> Military strategy scholars claim that the best, most thoroughly planned battle strategies are often abandoned ten minutes into the fight. The same concept applies to Lamaze class. After her first contraction, the wife will forget anything she learned in class and beg for drugs. Count on it.

YOUR EVOLVING VOCABULARY

<u>Word or Expression:</u> **COLIC / COWLICK**

Old Meaning:

> Either:
>
> a) The potentially fatal consequence of a horse that has eaten wet hay; or
>
> b) The point on the head where a person's hair swirls together, thus accounting for the majority of one's "bad hair" days.

New Meaning:

> The all-encompassing reason why your kid writhes in pain, screams all day and night, and keeps you and your wife at the very end of your respective ropes. Don't even bother asking what it is or what causes colic. Just rest (albeit briefly) assured that your child will eventually "outgrow" it. In the meantime, if he's really got it, you're in for a hellish run.
>
> Generally, it is our semi-expert opinion that the terms "colic" and "colicky" are grossly overused with infants, much like "ADHD" in older children. For example, if a twelve year old bounces off the walls all day and gets crappy grades, she *must* have ADHD. (Forget the fact that she is unsupervised and regularly drinks a six-pack of Coke before noon.) Similarly, if your infant is screaming bloody murder, your wife will calmly explain, "Oh, don't worry, honey. Tommy's just 'colicky' again." In making her expert medical analysis, she will tend

to overlook the fact that the dog just digested the kid's pacifier.

Word or Expression: **COLD ONE**
Old Meaning:
> A refreshing icy beverage, usually a frosty beer. Context: *Hey, Hank, pass me a cold one!*

New Meaning:
> A frigid night spent in the minivan. Of course, Hank will be nowhere in sight as you seek isolated refuge from your wife, kids, or both. On the bright side, a "cold one" affords you the opportunity for quality bonding time with Fido.

Word or Expression: **SIPPY**
Old Meaning:
> A term used by someone who may have imbibed a few too many sip(pie)s. This expression would never be used by anyone with a blood alcohol level of less than .25%. Context: *Really, ossiffer, I had nothing to drink at the party…Well, I take that back – maybe just a sippy or two.*

New Meaning:
> A virtually unbreakable, unspillable plastic cup with a screw-on top used for kid's drinks. You'll wind up buying at least five sippies per child. We'd love to have the patent on this simple but effective little device. And don't be surprised when your child insists that the color of the cup match perfectly

with that of the lid, or he will refuse to drink what's inside. Talk about being held hostage. This can be especially challenging in the dark as you retrieve the kid's sippy at 5 a.m.

Word or Expression: **SLEEP LIKE A BABY**
Old Meaning:
A state of blissful incoherence. *Two six packs later, I was out like a light, sleepin' like a baby.*
New Meaning:
An oxymoronic metaphor, like *soar like a turtle* or *cheat like a saint*. Babies are like bats; they only sleep during daylight hours, while you're at work, or so you are told.

Word or Expression: **BIG GIRL / BIG BOY**
Old Meaning:
(Noun) A nice way of referring to an individual who is rather large. Context: *She's a big girl, but she's got a wonderful personality.*
New Meaning:
(Adjective) A descriptive expression used to characterize something that is typically used by "older" children (for example, a big girl cup or a big boy bed). This expression is usually used to coerce or convince your youngster that he or she is ready to graduate from the baby version (in this case, the sippy or crib) to the "big kid" version (a normal plastic cup or twin bed). You will thank your lucky

stars when your child finally gives up diapers and advances to "big boy" underwear.

Word or Expression: **BLANKIE**
Old Meaning:
A period during which nothing happens, such as a scoreless inning or an unsuccessful date.
New Meaning:
A child's blanket. Like Linus in the Peanuts cartoon, your child and his or her "blankie" may be inseparable. To some kids, their blanket offers security and becomes as important to them as, say, a credit card is to an adult. God help you if you ever lose or misplace your child's old frayed blankie. Don't even think of trying to replace it; your little one will *instantly* recognize a shoddy imitation.

Word or Expression: **COMMUTE**
Old Meaning:
A dreadful period (usually 30 – 90 minutes, twice a day) spent traveling from home to work, and vice versa. For most people, it is common for anxiety and blood pressure to skyrocket as they sit in traffic. In prolonged cases, built-up frustration can result in extreme actions, such as road rage.
New Meaning:
Once you become a new father, it will not take you long to realize that the commute is the greatest part of your day. No screaming. No crying. No one

pulling at your limbs or clothes. Silence, or better yet, *your* music. If there is no one you *want* to speak to, shut off your cell phone and relax! During your daily commute, **you** *actually have control!* Control of the temperature. Control of the windows. Control of your destination and any requisite "pit stops." A man with foresight will find a way to *increase* his commute, either by moving farther from the office or by finding a job two counties away, *before* having children.

As usual, we have no scientific data for support, but we suspect that young fathers are very rarely involved in anything resembling road rage. To the extent that one might be, his role would likely be as a victim rather than aggressor, as he cuts in front of somebody while dozing off. Generally, the commuting new father is way too relaxed to get pissed.

Word or Expression: **CO-PAYMENT**
Old Meaning:

Before children arrive, and barring serious illness or injury at a young age, it is unlikely that you will have had any exposure to this insidious term. No need to worry. Soon, it will be more common than a grocery bill.

New Meaning:
> Though they may initially appear benign enough, your medical co-payments will quickly constitute a major household expense. Yeah, 10% of a child's medical bill or a flat fee of $20/visit is not much. But multiply it by the number of times per month each kid gets dragged to the doctor, multiplied by number of kids, and you get a big "after tax" figure. Quickly. On top of that, add your deductible for medicines. You'll be buying calls on health care stocks before you know it!

Word or Expression: **GENIE**
Old Meaning:
> As in "I Dream Of…" Larry Hagman. Barbara Eden. Enough said.

New Meaning:
> Genie, as in Diaper Genie. A pseudo-appliance soon to become at least as important as your beloved garbage disposal.

Word or Expression: **BLOWOUT**
Old Meaning:
> Either:
>> a) What happens (usually at the worst possible time) to the tire(s) on your car; or

YOUR EVOLVING VOCABULARY

> b) What can occur at a sporting event. A blow-out can be messy if your team is on the "receiving" end.

New Meaning:
> Any way you look at it, the "new" blow-out is messy. Basically, this is what transpires when too much matter is quickly injected into too little space. The results can be catastrophic. You will rightfully wonder how a tiny child who barely eats anything can generate that much matter with such force. The first time it happens with your kid, you'll think it was a sonic boom. Just hope it never occurs somewhere quiet, like in a library or a church. Very embarrassing.
>
> Cleaning up the resultant mess is not for the faint of heart. For the newly initiated father, rubber gloves, a nose plug, and a roll of paper towels are recommended. And, for God's sake, get the kid off the carpet as quickly as possible. If the wife's away, the garden hose and a pressure nozzle can come in handy, too.

<u>Word or Expression:</u> **MURPHY'S LAW**
Old Example:
> A steward's inquiry reverses the order of finish in the third race at the track, thus erasing your big exacta hit. Or, for you non-horseracing fans, your team

stages a dramatic, once-in-a-lifetime comeback 10 minutes after you left the game to beat the traffic.

New Example:

Anything you say which is in any way obscene, derogatory, or otherwise inappropriate will be repeated by your toddler at the worst possible moment.

<u>Word or Expression:</u> **VACATION**

Old Meaning:

Think Spring Break. Sun, Sand, Surf, Sodom, Gomorrah.

New Meaning:

Think overloaded minivan. Think misery. Mayhem. Detention. It has been suggested by more than one of our "contributors" that, in a woman's eyes, the "ideal" male is either a bellhop or a sherpa. The theory certainly holds up in the case of the "family vacation" (this term, by the way, will soon be added to your list of favorite oxymorons, right behind "jumbo shrimp" and "pretty ugly").

Much will be discussed about vacations in Chapter 13. Until then, however, consider buying yourself a hitch and a trailer for the family vehicle. And when packing the trailer, leave a little spot for yourself, lest things in the minivan get out of control and you need a quiet break.

YOUR EVOLVING VOCABULARY

<u>Word or Expression:</u> **SUCCESS**

Old Meaning:

> While growing up, the term *success* takes on different meanings at various stages in one's personal development. A child's goal, for instance, might be to become a doctor, a professional athlete, or even President of the United States. A high school student might define success as being rich and famous. For many a college student, success lies in earning passing grades, getting laid, and drinking large quantities of beer as quickly as possible. For the married guy who has yet to experience the joys of fatherhood, success is defined by holding down a good job, keeping a nice home, and building a family with his new bride (who is still a nymphomaniac).

New Meaning:

> For the married guy with an infant or toddler, success means getting four hours of uninterrupted sleep, holding on to a crappy job, seeing a movie in a theater more than once a year, and staying the hell out of Chuck E. Cheese's. The Pinnacle of Success is reached by the young father who somehow manages to avoid the purchase of any vehicle with a sliding door (it *is* OK to *rent* a minivan while on "vacation.").

<u>Word or Expression:</u> **WATCH** (verb)
Old Meaning:

>Watch, as in:
>>Watch a ballgame.
>>>Watch the sun set.
>>>>Watch paint dry.

>The point is that it is a *passive* activity and can be done at a distance. Both of these key elements will change quickly when kids arrive.

New Meaning:

>>Watch, as in:
>>>Watch a child.

>Contrary to what you might think, watching your kid is *not* a passive activity, and *don't even think* about doing it from afar. Men may be from Mars and women from Venus, but their ideas on "watching" children are solar systems apart. Always beware of potential "interpretive discrepancies" between what your wife is "saying" and what you might be "hearing." For example, when she says she's "stepping out" and asks that you "watch" your two children,

YOUR EVOLVING VOCABULARY

What she *means* is:

> *"For an indefinite period of time, I demand that you follow both children around, never venturing more than 24" away from either. Make sure they keep their hands off everything and each other, don't trip or fall down, and remain inside the house at all times, preferably on a soft surface. If, at any point, they need anything, fulfill their needs as expediently and efficiently as possible, never taking your eyes off them. If either of them so much as looks like she might sneeze, take both to the doctor immediately."*

What you *hear* is:

> *"Between innings, just glance over and make sure the kids aren't swallowing rat poison. They can yell, scream, and jump around, so long as they don't knock over your beer, step in your bean dip, or otherwise impair your enjoyment of the game. If you smell something funny, just make sure it stays in the diaper. I'll change them when I return, which will be very soon."*

Chapter 9

"The In-Laws Are Coming, The In-Laws are Coming!"

"If your baby is 'beautiful and perfect, never cries or fusses, sleeps on schedule and burps on demand, an angel all the time,' you're the grandma."
-- Theresa Bloomingdale

Before the arrival of kids in your household, it's usually not too tough to deal with your wife's parents. Yeah, while dating, you probably had to creatively market yourself as a gentle, caring, thoughtful and responsible young man with an obviously bright future. You might have even had to coerce your future father-in-law into forking over some dough for the wedding. And since then, you've probably had to endure a murderously boring family gathering or two. But as long as they don't live across the street (a la "Everybody Loves Raymond"), your pre-parental exposure to the in-laws is usually:
a) limited, b) controllable, and c) tolerable.

Items a, b, and c change drastically once Mom and Junior come home from the hospital. That first post-birth, pre- Red Zone visit by the wife's folks can be the toughest. Of course you'll initially welcome the extra help; but after about two weeks or so, you will start to wonder if and when they will ever leave. And once they finally do take off, your break will be short-lived. You see, now the in-laws have a *legitimate* reason to show up on a moment's notice and disrupt your tenuous hold on sanity: to see their grandchild!

Through our research and interviews, it appears that many grandparents spend more time and attention on their grandkids than they did on their own children; it's almost as if they're trying to make up for their past mistakes. Which is nice, except for the fact that grandparents enjoy a luxury that parents do not – they can come and go when they please. You will rue the day that Grandpa slips little Johnny a Pixie Stick. The act is kind and innocent enough, but when the kid starts bouncing off the walls and tumbling across the furniture, *Grandpa and Grandma can split*. It'll be just you and your wife, trying to control a crazed badger until his blood sugar level returns to earth a few hours later.

Some other random observations relating to grandparents, their grandchildren, and relatives in general:

- Be especially careful about buying or renting too much space. In-laws are attracted to spare bedrooms like rust to metal. It's that "nature hates a void" thing. And worse yet, you'll wind up hosting the entire family for their holiday gatherings – your home or apartment will become the "default" destination for all the relatives and their screaming kids!

- You've never seen so much junk until you see what's given to your children at Christmas or for any of their

"THE IN-LAWS ARE COMING, THE IN-LAWS ARE COMING!"

birthdays. Unbelievable. At least when you celebrate at Aunt Irma's, you can chuck the crap out of your car on the way home. There is, however, a bright side to having your home serve as the family dumping ground: your nearby Salvation Army, a worthy organization, will become the primary beneficiary. Even more important, you get a valuable tax write-off. Note: You might want to establish a "garbage in, garbage out" pact with your wife; for every piece of new crap that finds its way into the house, another has to be given away (the outgoing junk is usually last year's gifts).

- When *your* parents are visiting, things can get really dicey if you're not careful. Keep a watchful eye on the topics of conversation that either of them has with your wife. If they piss her off, she will take it out on you later. Similarly, your wife will hold you accountable for any lax behavioral latitude that your folks have given your kids during their stay. For example, your mother might allow the kid to play in the yard or eat unwashed fruit. These unforgivable actions will be your fault and will become your problems.

- <u>Never</u> assume that your relatives are actually watching your children, even when they claim to be doing so. This is especially true when the little ones are eating. Unless the food they throw is the size of a watermelon, Grandma is not likely to notice. (You will find this especially curious since, when the kids are at Grandma's house, she'll catch a tossed raisin before it hits the floor!)

Finally, since this book is intended as a "survival guide," we have endeavored to provide several combat tactics to counterattack repeated assaults on the home front (in plain English, we want to give you some practical methods of getting rid of visiting in-laws). Importantly, any such operations must be undertaken covertly. If your wife catches on to the fact that you're purposely trying to scare her family off, you'll wind up more miserable than if you'd just endured their visit in the first place.

COMBAT TACTICS:
1. Perform a controlled rodent release in the guest bedroom.
2. After taking your shower, turn off the gas valve on the hot water heater.
3. After inserting your trusty earplugs and just prior to retiring to bed, slip a dead battery into the smoke alarm. The loud chirp every twenty seconds will send the in-laws running for cover.
4. Get one of your friends who owns a Harley to remove the muffler and pay you a "surprise" early morning visit. When quizzed as to his motivations, have him claim to be on his way to some sort of charity ride – they always seem to start early.

"THE IN-LAWS ARE COMING, THE IN-LAWS ARE COMING!"

5. Slip your gardener an extra twenty bucks to set up camp just outside the guest bedroom window with his collection of weedwackers, leaf blowers, and other noisy, gas-powered noise polluting devices.

Chapter 10

Clothing Your Toddler: Focus on the Bare Necessities

"It sometimes happens, even in the best of families, that a baby is born. This is not necessarily cause for alarm. The important thing is to keep your wits about you and borrow some money."
-- Elinor Goulding Smith

Few things in your life will constitute a bigger waste of time than dealing with children's clothing. Buying outfits, constantly washing them with special "kid-friendly" soap, folding them, struggling to put them on a squirming kid…waste, waste, waste! Unfortunately, like the diaper dilemma, there's just no way around it. There are, however, things you can do as an Enlightened Dad in order to simplify the process.

To begin with, it will help if you address the clothing issue in the right frame of mind. Remember your wedding? If you were like most mentally-functioning males, your initial enthusiasm for planning the details of the event quickly faded to an attitude of "I don't give a damn. Just tell me what I owe and get me to the honeymoon." The same general concept applies here. Take it from us – your wife and her female friends are the only ones who will care about the clothing your kid wears. (Note: Our limited research shows this theory to hold true until your child reaches age 3, at which time he too will care and will incorporate even less logic into the process than your wife and her gabbing friends.)

Be objective; take a step back and watch the clothes follies. You will be reminded of those people who think it's cute to dress up their dog or cat and parade it around town. Let's face it – your toddler gives not a rat's ass about the color, style, or brand name on his clothing. Don't think for a second that Junior gets any more utility from wearing Baby Gap than he would outfitted in something pulled from the "50 cents" pile at the local swap meet. And don't fall for the quality argument. The kid will outgrow said garment before the first signs of wear are noticeable under a microscope. By the time he would "hand it down" to his younger sibling, it will likely be either "out of style" or irreparably stained. No, the only people who care about toddler's clothing are parents, and more specifically, moms.

Of course, the biggest joke of any clothing item worn by toddlers are those frilly headbands parents love to slap on their unsuspecting daughters' heads. What, is the kid having problems with hair in her eyes? Sweat? Are the parents trying to prep the kid for a career in the WNBA? Gentlemen, do society (and yourself) a favor – when the wife's not looking, lose the head garters. Your daughter will grow up faster than you think, and she'll soon be thanking you every time she looks back at the family photos. And while we're on the subject, don't *ever* put a bow tie on your little boy until he's old enough to return the favor and hit you back.

Be grateful for any baby clothes you receive before the egg is hatched – be they given out of obligation at a baby shower,

CLOTHING YOUR TODDLER:
FOCUS ON THE BARE NECESSITIES

or out of sympathy as your friends notice you beginning to realize the size of the safe which is about to land on your head. Remember: gifts are good – less stuff to buy after D-day. And be prepared – your first solo visit to one of those "A-list" infant clothing stores will send you into shock. You'll think the clerk errantly put the decimals in the wrong place on the price tags. Though it is typically made with a fraction of the material in adult clothing, brand name infant apparel often costs much more. This harsh discovery will bring you back to the realization that the only ones who really care about toddler fashion are moms. You will then proceed directly back to your beloved couch in order to watch football and convince yourself that the money you intend to save will be better "invested" in a satellite hook-up.

Insofar as we're concerned, there are only two articles of clothing necessary for the youngest of kids: the t-shirt and the one-piece pajamas.

First, the t-shirt. From a visual perspective, you're presented with a wide array of options. You can buy little t-shirts with your college name, your favorite team, or a surf wear logo. You can also take the humorous approach, letting Junior wear a shirt which reads something like, "Check out my mom's hooters" on the front, or "If you are reading this shirt, dad dressed me" on the back.

From a purely functional standpoint, t-shirts are completely adequate. If it's too cold for a t-shirt, the kid should be in his pajamas. And who really cares if you can see a kid's diaper? We all know he's wearing one, so why hide it with a pair of shorts or a onesie? Before they inevitably get lost, toddlers' shorts tend to get very dirty. And while easy to remove, onesies will drive you bananas as you try to line up 36 pairs of snaps while putting them on your writhing child. So until Proctor & Gamble comes out with a Velcro onesie, stick with the diaper / t-shirt combination. And who cares if you hear someone mutter "trailer trash" under his or her breath? You just saved yourself a ton of time and money, not to mention your own sanity!

The other clothing necessity for your toddler is the one-piece pajama with slippers built in. These simple little garments can be practically worn year-round, since kids rarely complain about being too hot. Most moms get their young kids accustomed to abnormally high body temperatures by making them wear ski parkas in July. As a father, you are far more likely to get grief from your wife for dressing the kids too lightly (lest they get "chilled") than for dressing them too warmly. Stick with the pajamas, and you'll never be accused of neglect.

An interesting thing with young kids is that they often have absolutely no idea how to stay under their covers when sleeping. To them, a blanket is just another thing to clutter the bed and hide their stuffed animals. Neatly tuck in your toddler, come back twenty minutes later, and see just how deluded you were. Our advice: leave the blankets in the closet and, again, rely on the pajamas.

CLOTHING YOUR TODDLER: FOCUS ON THE BARE NECESSITIES

The only downside with young kids' pajamas concerns the built-in slippers. While it can be funny to watch, kids sliding around on hard-surfaced floors can have a cruel twist that may result in an expensive trip to the local ER. You'd think that a couple of headers while rounding the same corner might slow them down, but their learning curve isn't as steep as Darwin would have you believe. To combat this fact, try to find pajamas that have sticky or padded rubber surfaces on the bottoms of the slippers.

Beside your two necessary staples – the t-shirt and pajamas – the only other article of clothing you might want to consider is a good little pair of overalls. They have a couple features that make them especially attractive to the impatient dad. First, they can be worn by either boys or girls (which also make them great hand-me-downs). And second, they will allow you to move your child short distances very quickly – just carry the kid like a six-pack.

Once Junior starts walking, his clothing needs start to expand rapidly. To begin with, he needs shoes, which will present a sizable hurdle to his parents when they are trying to leave the house in a hurry. Hint: For *your* child's first few pairs of shoes, *don't even consider* buying those with laces (buying lace-up shoes for someone else's kid is OK, especially if that "someone else" or their kid is especially annoying). Once again, Velcro rules. It's fast, easy, and the learning curve is fairly flat (your kid will learn how to put his shoes on and take them off in a relatively short period of time). Unfortunately, this will probably not solve all your problems. Since toddlers' shoes are so short, it's often difficult to tell the right shoe from the left. As a general rule, if your child yells in pain immediately after you've stuck his shoes on, consider switching them. Once things have settled down, grab a Sharpie and mark each shoe with an "R" or "L".

Another interesting aspect of little shoes is that they possess one of the greatest unexplained forces in nature – the ability to suck sand out of a playground from distances up to about 50 feet. If this phenomenon were fully understood, we're convinced that you could vacuum your entire house with one pair of baby Nikes. But until that day, prepare yourself for the inevitable dumpage of sand on your clean floors. You'll welcome your child home from pre-school, remove one of his shoes, and "Blam!" – more sand will fall out of the shoe than you ever thought possible. And how a little foot and that much sand managed to simultaneously fit into one little shoe is an even greater mystery.

As children grow, they will demand to have more input into their daily attire. Generally speaking, this is a good thing. It saves time and gives you an out when your wife interrogates you as to why the blue Superman shirt is paired with the lime green sweat pants. In some cases, it gets to the point where, fearing the clothing combinations that dad or the child might come up with, mom will actually lay out the specific clothes she wants the kid to wear. If this happens to you, pretend you didn't see the pre-selected, perfectly matching outfit, and dress

CLOTHING YOUR TODDLER: FOCUS ON THE BARE NECESSITIES

your toddler like you always do. If mom wants Junior to wear specific clothes, she should put them on herself.

Lastly, when you find yourself losing yet another kid-related clothing argument, remember this inquiry as a way to divert the discussion: "Honey, what good is that cute $80 rain jacket on Sally when you never let her go out in the rain?"

Chapter 11

Freedom

"Raising kids is part joy and part guerilla warfare."
-- Ed Asner

It is difficult for any author to write meaningfully about a subject to which he has no exposure. Such is our dilemma. After years of raising infants and now toddlers, neither of us is in much of a position to speak about the virtues of freedom. We basically have none. Accordingly, this chapter is relatively short. We do, however, have several suggestions that might enable you to squeeze out a few precious moments for yourself over the next few years. These pearls of wisdom are revealed on the pages that follow and, when added to the tactics covered in Chapter 7, should provide you adequate means to maintain your mental stability. But beware: moments of freedom and personal bliss will be few and far between, and finding them will require cunning and creative action on your part. Long gone are the impromptu Vegas junkets, as well as the all-night poker soirees with all the trimmings. Proceed with caution, Dad!

"Free at last, free at last, thank God almighty, I'm free at last!"
-- Martin Luther King, Jr.

Throughout the first year of fatherhood, you may frequently find yourself muttering these very words while pulling your car out of the garage (solo, of course). Though our new use of this memorable quote is substantially different than its original intent, believe us, these words will take on new meaning and significance as you head off to work after a three-day weekend spent at home with the family. For reasons having nothing to do with your employer (other than the fact that you're occasionally allowed to spend silent time at your desk), you might find yourself, for the first time, *eager* to get to work. Your office may actually become a sort of "haven," a personal "port in the storm."

Before having young children, we were baffled at why people would take jobs in fields like business consulting or national sales, which require that employees spend weeks, sometimes months, away from home. Now, either of us will leap at any opportunity to take a business trip, whether it be to Tucson or Toledo. The fact is that every city in the United States has nice, clean hotel rooms, where it's actually *against house rules* to make noise and prevent other visitors from a good night's sleep. Other perks include room service and non-Disney movies. It's heavenly.

As alluded to earlier, battles for attaining moments of freedom will be hard fought. One of the keys to earning (albeit short) periods of "personal time" will lie in your ability to learn to focus. For example, you will often need to block out screaming kids, a barking dog, a ringing phone, and blaring Barney music in order to maintain the focus and concentration necessary to get the key scores from SportsCenter. But be patient. Focus of this magnitude does not develop overnight.

FREEDOM

Your waning personal freedom can be best illustrated by looking no farther than your beloved car. Just as that wedding ring on your finger has come to represent the ball, chain, and airbrakes on your free-swinging bachelorhood, so your kid's car seat will come to symbolize what (little) is left of your freedom. Yeah, the baby seat is an essential accessory and, indeed, is probably the best safety device ever developed. But any man who has ever had to schlep his dog down to the vet to be neutered will know the feeling of strapping a car seat into his fossil fuel burning pride and joy. The (formerly) beautiful machine will not only appear sad, lonely, and instantly become less cool to look at, but it will suddenly handle more poorly and get worse gas mileage. And that's *before* it starts filling up with cracker crumbs, pretzel parts, and sticky juice remnants.

Try as you might, you really can't get around keeping a car seat in place full time. Fighting the industry is admirable, but stupid. Here's what will happen: some sunny Saturday, your wife will have a commitment, and you'll be "in charge" of the kid for the day (while conducting our research, several women informed us that it is not "correct" to say that a father "babysits" his own child). You'll play with your little guy and successfully entertain him for a few hours, then you'll start itching for a little drive to the hardware store. Or maybe it's McDonald's. Or maybe the magazine stand. Hell, anywhere as long as it's out of the house. You'll cruise out to the car, open the door, and freeze in horror. No car seat! It's in the *other* car! Your brain will scream a word or three that your mouth has been sworn not to mutter in front of the kid. In theory, this shouldn't be such a crisis; you just turn around and try to get the kid to become a fan of whatever happens to be on ESPN. In reality, however, you quickly come to the accurate conclusion that you are a prisoner. The only way you're getting out is by pushing that floral-patterned, wobbly-wheeled stroller the mile and a half to the store, then back again.

But this book is not intended as a downer. It's all about optimism, solutions, and survival. Our mission is to help you acquire more freedom, or at least to hold its decline at bay. In attempting to accomplish this, one battle-tested tactic we've run across is the establishment and successful maintenance of a personal "time slot." Learn from the experiences of Greg, a seasoned father of three:

> *Like many young fathers, I was always exhausted on Monday mornings. After squeezing in yard work and honey-do's while taking care of the kids, there was never any time left to do the things I wanted or needed to do. In retrospect, my marriage suffered, as did my relationship with my children.*
>
> *My solution was to establish my own "time slot." Each Saturday morning, I would "go exercise" from seven until ten. At first, my wife protested, but before too long, she grew to get used to it, expected it, and accepted it. Fact is, often I didn't even exercise at all. Sometimes,*

I'd go to the park and take a nap on a bench or under a tree. Other times, I'd visit my favorite greasy spoon and read the morning paper. When I returned home to face the battle, I was rejuvenated, better able to actually enjoy the kids and thrive in the chaos. Eventually, I had to provide my wife with a time slot of her own, but she often forgot to use it or cut it short. Though she never admitted it, she seemed to possess limited confidence in my ability to supervise and control three wild toddlers while watching a football game.

The personal "time slot" practice executed by Greg is a wonderful concept. The key to it, however, is to be <u>disciplined</u>. Remember, you must *use it,* or you will *lose it.* Consistency is critical. Think of it like you would an expense budget at work.

Chapter 12

High (Chair) Fashion

"The other night I ate at a real nice family restaurant.
Every table had an argument going."
-- **George Carlin**

Feeding kids is a trip…

It all starts with the infant needing his mother's milk. After an inconsistent start, he'll get into a groove and want it regularly throughout the day, regardless of his parents' work, social, or sleep schedules. And there isn't really a whole lot that you, as the dad, can do. Basically, when Junior starts crying at around 3 am, you'll need to roll over, elbow your wife, and mutter something like "Honey, I'd love to help, but…" And to take full advantage of this biological perk, make sure your wife breastfeeds for a long time, like until the kid is four. Remember, every meal sucked from the Momma Café is one less meal you're involved in, either physically, emotionally, or financially. And diaper stench will take a sharp turn for the worse once the kid is off the breast.

Contrary to what you might think, not all moms dig breastfeeding. It's not comfortable. It's not convenient. Blah blah blah. Your wife will come up with every reason in the book to start trying to get you involved in this chore, but stick to your guns and have some good arguments in the chamber. Counter with lines like "kids that breast feed are more likely to develop better immunities to germs," or "think of the powerful bonding you're developing by such a natural feeding style," or maybe "have you seen how flippin' expensive formula is?" (all defendable and thoroughly-researched points).

No matter how well the battle is waged, at some point the kid will need to start eating from a fork or spoon. This is when things start to get interesting. Assuming that your kid doesn't mind the taste of liquefied veggies (and if he does, this will eventually change), the most obvious challenge is actually getting the food into the hungry mouth (It's even more challenging getting food into a non-hungry mouth). Visualize trying to thread a needle with oven mitts on, after you've had several shots of tequila. Kids have the same problem directing hands and eating utensils to their mouths. The coordination just isn't there, and the result is usually messy.

As your child matures, there is often a brief transition period of gut-busting humor. Junior will want to feed himself, and initially, this will be a great and frequent source of laughter for you and your wife. It's fun to watch them paint themselves carrot-orange or shove small vegetables into new-found facial orifices. Keep the camera handy in these early days, 'cause once they're gone, they're gone.

But again, this period is brief. And just like getting the same e-mailed joke over and over, cleaning up after a nuclear lunch gets old. The amazement of "how the hell did food get under *there*?" quickly segues into "I gotta get to work. Gimme that spoon!"

Some of the most frustrating meals are often those that occur after the child actually has the eating thing figured out. Kids don't operate under the same schedule as parents. They don't have to get to a job by a certain time. They don't have to get to Home Depot or Costco before the fleet of SUVs rolls in. They don't have to get anywhere—by any time. As far as they're concerned, they have all day to eat that bowl of Cheerios. And it's hard to get a kid to eat fast. Real hard. Salvation comes in the form of the old adage: "They won't starve themselves," and it's true (no matter how sound the argument, mothers still don't buy it). This leads to another new experience: throwing away piles of perfectly good food. It will take a while, but eventually 30% of your diet will be eating kid scraps, like three bites of cereal here, 5 grapes there, and an occasional PB&J leftover nightcap.

Some helpful tips:

- Get the biggest bibs you can buy and insist the kid wear them until they reach high school. Better yet, train them to eat in the nude and reduce your laundry load by 50%.
- Stick a painter's drop cloth under Junior's chair. It won't look so great, but it will look better than the three-day old macaroni and cheese dropping that needs to be chiseled off the floor.

- If the little guy wants to mix ketchup with his milk, let him. He's gonna come up with some unbelievable food combinations, and some he'll actually eat.
- Let the dog sleep under the table.
- Always have a clean mop and a working vacuum at the ready.
- Watch out for the random cough or sneeze. Because of the lack of audible warning, you'll get good at identifying the "feed me" open mouth vs. the "here it comes" open mouth, usually after you get a spoonful of whipped peas blown all over your monkey suit. (Even after the meal, thoroughly inspect yourself after a good kid sneeze. It's embarrassing to get to the office and have someone exclaim, "Hey Bob, is that a night crawler on your shoulder?")
- Beware of boxed juices. Somehow scientists have recreated an atmospheric imbalance inside the box so that as soon as the kid gets the beverage into their grasp, half the stain-prone liquid is shot up through the straw and all over the back seat of your car. Drink the first 20% yourself before handing over these juice bombs to your little one. Better yet, "pop the wings" on top of the box to lessen the pressure differential.

Chapter 13

<u>*Getting Out of Town:*</u>
<u>*The Family "Detention"*</u>

"The truth is that parents are not really interested in justice. They just want quiet."
-- Bill Cosby

The concept of vacationing with young children really challenges the meaning and purpose of the term "vacation." <u>Webster's Dictionary</u> defines a vacation as "a time set aside from work, study, etc., for recreation or rest; a holiday." Hmm.

Since whatever you will be doing and/or enduring while on "vacation" with kids differs so drastically from the definition of the term, we felt it important to come up with a new expression that more accurately describes this activity. So just like the guy who sang "Little Red Corvette" is the *Artist Formerly Known as Prince*, that time spent with the family in Hawaii might now be coined *The Time Period Formerly Known as a Vacation*. Because this is too long of an expression, and TPFKAV is a cumbersome acronym, we will, from this point forward, refer to this time period as a *detention*. Similarly, the act (read: grave error) of engaging in this activity will be known as "*detentioning*."

A word to the wise: if your first child is still on the way and you enjoy vacationing, you better get it out of your system, and quick. Take a five-week boat trip up the Nile River without getting your shots. Explore the remote regions of China sans luggage, cash, or credit cards. Parade the streets of Baghdad wearing an Uncle Sam tuxedo. In short, do whatever is necessary to ensure yourself a lousy, miserable time. By the end of this exercise, you should never want to leave home again. Take this advice and, once children arrive, you'll have the proper response when your wife comes up with the brilliant idea of heading to Puerta Vallarta with your two young toddlers. To quote Nancy Reagan in an entirely different context, "Just Say No!"

The logic employed behind these ideas may not be fully understood by any father who has not yet experienced the pleasure of detentioning with his family. Even he with a trip or two under his belt might think we've really blown it on this one. "My child is perfect," he'll say. "She's so low maintenance – she sleeps all the time…blah, blah, blah." Maybe. You may indeed have a good trip, maybe even a "vacation," right out of the gate. But sooner or later, your world is going to teeter and then topple. As we all know from our road trips to Vegas in our former lives, the odds eventually catch up with you. You will come to hate the very sound of words like "trip," "travel," and "vacation," preferring instead to stay at home where toys are plentiful, friends can't hear your kids scream, and you're never more than three short strides from another cold Corona.

Detentioning is nothing like any activity you've ever experienced. With all respect due Mr. Webster, it is *not* a time away from work, study, etc. It is no time for recreation or

GETTING OUT OF TOWN:
THE FAMILY "DETENTION"

rest. And believe us, it bears no resemblance whatsoever to a holiday.

A vacation was a time when you could recharge your batteries, redirect and re-energize yourself. In contrast, there is no "down time" while detentioning. Every day is scheduled, pre-planned down to the minute. No snoozing on the beach, no devouring a good book, no more sipping rum drinks poolside for hours on end. The spontaneous nookie session back in the hotel room will be a thing of the past. Since you'll be exhausted by sundown, late night partying will also quickly fade into distant memory. Rather, during your detention, your "free time" will now be found in ten-minute increments shoved in between baby feedings, naps, and diaper changes. You'll be required to do something you've never had to do before in paradise – *be responsible*. Believe us, nothing says paradise like stealing a passing glance at a beautiful sunset while cleaning up your kid's latest offering of butt soup. Gentlemen, Mr. Fun has left the building. Detentioning will be like getting a lap dance while your mother looks on – "This should be an awesome experience, but I can't wait 'til it's over!" Eventually, your ability to tolerate the suffering will break down, and you'll tread the path of many a man before you, begging your wife to take the kids, along with her parents, and go off on "vacation" without you. (Any man who actually manages to pull this off needs to get into a career in sales immediately.)

In the mean time, here is just a sampling of the concepts and ideas that you will learn while spending quality detention time with the family:

1. What it feels like to be a pack mule.
2. Taking kids on airplanes is a bad idea and should be illegal.
3. For the entire detention, your wife will worry that your child will somehow squeeze through the railing of a hotel balcony. FYI, most of these railings are so tight they could filter salt from seawater.
4. Kids have an entirely different take on "Happy Hour."
5. What it's like to be the most hated person on a commercial airplane (see #2).
6. Young children do not sleep too well in "new" environments (read: if the kid isn't sleeping, neither are you).
7. Traveling with a stroller is a necessary evil. Pushing the damn thing around while also toting baggage is difficult, but not nearly as tough as trying to carry the kid too (the luggage neither squirms nor screams). Learning to balance a duffel bag on a kid's head isn't too hard, but doing so without him crying is a real skill.

GETTING OUT OF TOWN:
THE FAMILY "DETENTION"

8. It's easier to teach a lizard to recite Shakespeare than to keep an awake and alert two-year old in his airplane seat for more than ten minutes.
9. Your house will never look so beautiful as it does after a seven-day detention.
10. Neither will your office.

In an attempt to maintain your dignity and your sanity, here are a few valuable tips:

- When driving to the airport, generously offer to drop your wife and children off at the curb *first*, thereby lessening their walk and saving everyone the hassle of loading into and unloading out of the shuttle bus. Acting as the family martyr, you will then park the car and take the shuttle solo. This stunt usually works only once, so make it good. What this tactic affords you is 30 extra minutes of peace and quiet – plenty of time to catch a quick cat nap, slam a martini or two, and psyche yourself up for the impending hell that awaits you. In the mean time, your wife has had to deal with suitcases, check-in, and overly excited kids. You might want to save that second martini for her.
- Whenever and wherever possible, fly Southwest Airlines. The general rule with airlines is that children under the age of two can fly free, provided they sit on your lap. Since Southwest doesn't assign seats, no one will ever know if you bought a ticket for your kid or not. Just pre-board (this is actually the one

perk associated with detentioning with kids – take advantage of it!), stick your little love-bundle in a seat, and if anyone asks, just tell them his ticket is paid for. It may still be a long, miserable flight, but at least you will have saved some dough without having to travel with a little monster on your lap.

- Insist that your child take a healthy dose of allergy medicine before any flight. Under normal circumstances, something like Benadryl usually does the trick. If extreme measures are required, try a drop or two of Nyquil. This tends to take a little wind out of their sails and puts a little breeze in yours.
- Kill two birds with one stone and buy an infant seat that snaps on to a collapsible stroller frame.
- Avoid destinations that will require you to do a lot of driving. Find a hotel on the beach or a condo with direct access to the ski slopes. Spend the extra dough now, thank us later. Having to constantly gather kid supplies for (rental) car travel, getting the car seat ready, hoping the kid doesn't go to sleep in the car, etc…all these miserable activities will threaten to reduce or eliminate any remaining "fun" periods you might otherwise enjoy.
- While preparing for any detention, pack for yourself as lightly as possible. Be assured that you will be carrying much more than your stuff (see #1 above).
- Make sure your suitcases all have functioning wheels, so as to minimize the effort in transporting 800 pounds of luggage.

GETTING OUT OF TOWN: THE FAMILY "DETENTION"

- As soon as your kids are old enough to walk, make them carry backpacks and pull miniature suitcases with wheels. For practice and in preparation for any upcoming detention, load them up with rocks around the house. This practice will build both muscles and character.

Our best advice is to avoid detentions all together. Stay at home and fix something; at least you'll be productive. Bank your vacation days at work. Save your money. Start a "detention fund." This way, when the day finally arrives when your children are potty trained, able to walk and talk, and sleep in their own bed (at least part of the night), you'll be able to enjoy a "real" vacation.

Chapter 14

Birthday Parties in the New Millennium

"A truly appreciative child will break, lose, spoil, or fondle to death any really successful gift within a matter of minutes."
-- Russell Lynes

"Why birthday parties in the New Millennium?" you ask. "Have things changed that much since when I was a kid?"

Good question. Long answer. We'll try to simplify.

In a word, *hellyesthey'vechanged*. And without knowing what dramatic changes have occurred in the customs and practices of the typical child's birthday party, you will go into battle ill-prepared and unprotected. Think of General Custer at Little Big Horn. In order to clarify our presentation of this important topic, we've broken the material and advice in this chapter into two major "sub-groups" – that which involves your toddler attending another child's birthday party and the Granddaddy of All Miserable Experiences, the art and practice of throwing your own kid's birthday celebration. Each has its own unique aspects and challenges, which we hope to address effectively in the balance of the chapter.

THE ENLIGHTENED DAD

Case 1: <u>Your kid gets invited to a friend's birthday party</u>

Think back twenty-five years or so. Shut your eyes and imagine your sweaty, swearing, cigar-chomping father reluctantly chauffeuring you and a group of your screaming little buddies to a friend's birthday party. Picture good ol' Dad, in your mind's eye, slowing the Ford Country Squire just enough so you and your friends could pile out of the station wagon without augering in to the pavement. Do you remember just praying that the end of the old man's golf round and subsequent visit to the "19th hole" would somehow coincide with the end of the birthday party, thus saving you and your friends the three mile hike home? Do you recall not being at all surprised when he never showed up?

If you took your dad's approach today, you'd be arrested for child abuse and endangerment. These days, not only is a father obligated to bring the minivan to a full stop, he's expected to actually attend the party along with his wife and kid(s). He's forced to strike up conversations with a bunch of equally disinterested guys, most of whom can't seem to stop staring at their watches. And finally, he must stay for the *entire* shindig, all the while attempting to remain awake, sober, and "happy." If this isn't a miserable way to spend a Sunday afternoon, we'd like to hear your ideas of worse. Kids get punished with "time-outs"; the modern father gets birthday party duty.

In fact, if you actually enjoy cleaning tootsie-pop goo out of hair, having your wife order you around (in front of her friends) like some sort of pathetic dog, and getting whacked in the crotch by a three year old who is futilely searching for the piñata, please skip to the next chapter. But if, like us, you hope to muddle your way through fatherhood while maintaining some shred of dignity (no matter how miniscule), then read on, man. As always, after learning the "hard way," we've come up with a few creative solutions for our loyal readers.

Our recommended tactics begin well before the actual party that you and the family are expected to attend. Possibly even days earlier. First, you will need to make your wife aware of all the "productive" things that you could be doing if you were only excused from the upcoming birthday sentence: plant daisies, clean the cars, pull weeds, paint the front door. Obviously, these "options" don't have to be real. The point is, to the extent that she is susceptible, the "seeds of guilt" will be planted in your wife's mind. She may not let you out of the gig, but you've built a critical foundation.

Next, when getting yourself dressed for the "big event," be sure to look as crappy as possible – greasy hair, dirty teeth, clothes that aren't close to matching. Deodorant is out of the question. At this point, it's important that you realize something. As a relatively new father, attending a birthday party represents your first opportunity to "shine" in front of your wife's new "friends" (since, like you, she doesn't get out much, her new cronies are usually the mothers of your child's friends). The fact is that you may be a complete loser, an absolute zero in every sense of the term, but you have likely been "sold" by your wife to this gaggle of yacking women as the ultimate husband and father, a veritable "Mr. Everything." It all has to do with "motherly competition" – the subtle jabs that the women throw at each other to convince themselves and others that theirs is the ultimate family existence.

You will want to quickly and efficiently dispel any notion that you or your family is in any way normal or even marginally functional. To that end, the quicker you can manage to offend anyone and everyone, the quicker your departure, and the less likely you'll be to ever have to endure this type of punishment again. Try walking into the party with an open beer. Find an idle television and turn on a game. Fall asleep. Read a magazine in the bathroom. Go off on some wild, politically sensitive tirade. Explain to a group of mothers, in detail, how you plan on breeding pit bulls for fun and profit—in your living room. Remember, you don't want these folks simply not to like you or, worse yet, to think you're just a little weird. You want them to be *afraid*, even *terrified* of you. It is only then that you can hope to earn your way out of the dreaded "birthday circuit."

Case 2: Hosting a Birthday Party

This is where things can get really tricky. It's one thing to get kicked out of someone else's house after strategically stepping in dog crap; it's another challenge entirely to keep the "cult" of birthday partygoers out of your own home. We have yet to interview a father who has successfully dodged having to host

BIRTHDAY PARTIES IN THE NEW MILLENNIUM

at least one birthday party for his toddler. We have, however, listened to those who have managed to minimize the pain, suffering, and collateral damage. The results of their tales are outlined below.

Like the issue of child safety, the idea of throwing a bash for your kid's birthday is likely to rear its ugly head while you and the wife are in bed, just before you manage to drift off to sleep. "Honey," she'll say, "you know little Johnny is turning one a month from Saturday. We really should have some kind of a party..."

Let it be said here that, ideally speaking, the kid's first birthday "party" should be an easy one. The simple solution: haul Johnny to some other kid's party (these parties happen in groups anyway), slap a coned hat on his little head, and snap a few shots of him smiling somewhere near the presents and cake. *Presto!* Years (or for that matter, weeks) later, who will ever know the difference? Certainly not Johnny! Actually pulling off this stunt is nearly impossible, unless your wife is on an extended business trip. And even then, success in its entirety is a long shot.

Speaking of business trips, the well-read, properly prepared father will have planned one of his own which happens to coincide with Johnny's birthday well before his wife's aforementioned request. If this doesn't work, he will have shrewdly planned a one-day family excursion to a favorite relative's house. The simple logic at work here is that: a) the chances of your wife throwing a toddler birthday party while you're out of town are nil, and b) how hard can it be to throw the party when it's not at your house, no little kids will come, and you're hanging out with your immediate family members, all of whom are in a good mood?

If all the above tactics fail, or when you are finally required to give in and host a group of twenty screaming children and their parents, please take note of the following:

- No matter the cost savings, *never* attempt to transport helium balloons yourself. It's simply a rookie mistake. Driving with one eye closed while eating a messy burrito is safer than cruising down the freeway while wrestling with a car-full of these insidious things. If and when you do finally arrive home safely, the thirty strings of ribbon to which each balloon is attached will have tangled into one gigantic knot. This is an inevitable phenomenon for which you will be blamed and yelled at mercilessly, since spousal anxieties just prior to these ridiculous parties run high anyway. Finally, before ordering the balloons, multiply the number you need by 1.3. Without fail, a large number of balloons will pop before the party starts, many while you are affixing them to something. If you've never had an over-inflated helium-filled balloon explode four inches from your nose, you are in for a real treat.

BIRTHDAY PARTIES IN THE
NEW MILLENNIUM

- Be aware that, just as attendance requirements at children's birthday parties have changed in recent years, so too have gift-giving practices. In the New Millennium, it is no longer enough simply to buy overpriced cake, ice cream, and balloons and host the screaming munchkins and their folks. No sir. In addition to abiding by these "traditional" rules, the modern host must supply a "gift bag" to any child who shows up. Amazingly, even the kids who flake on the party are sent a gift bag! As illustrated by our technical analysis below, this ensures that, at least from an economic standpoint, the modern kid's birthday party is bound never to break even.

Birthday Gifts: An Economic Analysis

Assumptions:

Number of children attending party: 20
Number of children who flake: 5

Incoming Revenue

Total number of birthday gifts received: 18 (3 of 5 who flaked still manage to drop off gifts)
Average value of gifts received: $10
Number of gifts immediately thrown away or given to Goodwill: 8
Net value of gifts received (and kept): $100

> Out-flowing Revenue
>
> Number of "Gift Bags" prepared: 25
> Average cost per gift bag: $5
> Net expenses for gift bags given to guests: $125
>
> **Net gift-related cash flow: <$25>***
>
> *Actual results may vary but are almost guaranteed to be in the red. And remember, not included in this figure are the base cost of the venue, a piñata, the cake, furniture and drywall repair, carpet cleaning, ER visit(s), etc.

- As these birthday parties begin to occur more frequently, take notice of the "BCDS" (Birthday Circuit Death Spiral) which follows. If a group of these parties occurs in succession, you will surely notice that each is slightly more extravagant than the last. For example, if Cody has an inflatable "Bouncy Jumper" at his party, little Sierra's birthday the following weekend will feature the "Super Bouncy Jumper." Similarly, the same petting zoo might be employed on successive Saturdays, but the second party will undoubtedly include a few more exotic farm animals. This is not because little Cody or Sierra gives a rat's ass about what's at their parties (beyond basic cake and presents, of course). Rather, what somehow becomes more important is that Sierra's mother has to outdo Cody's. Again, motherly competition rearing its ugly *cabeza*. If gone unchecked, this ridiculous

BIRTHDAY PARTIES IN THE NEW MILLENNIUM

spending and entertainment competition will go on until some kid's unsuspecting father opens the Visa bill and is forced to file Chapter 11.

- If at all possible, throw your kid's birthday party "off-site." Even with their parents present and watching, kids will destroy your house and its contents in the blink of an eye. Find a place that has either screwed the furniture to the floor or has large open areas. The obvious choice here, the "lowest common denominator" if you will, is Chuck E. Cheese's. Regardless of where you live, you're never far from a Chuck E. Cheese's. To call one of these establishments a restaurant (they do serve pizza) would be unfair to any legitimate eatery. Regardless, sooner or later, you'll have to enter one of their franchises. And the instant you walk through the front door, you'll see why C.E.C.'s is a terrible venue to host a birthday party. Kids love it, but any adult with a double-digit I.Q. will have all of his or her senses brutally assaulted. Noise, chaos, and germs reign. That they serve beer, though tasteless and expensive, should come as no surprise. You will be amazed at how many kids have the same birthday as your child, as Chuck E. Cheese himself (you have to wonder about the cleanliness of any establishment where the mascot is a rat!) wanders among the groups of party-goers. This place is truly Party Central – mass production style. Should you doubt our assessment of this establishment, when was the last time one of your co-workers pranced into the office proclaiming, "Boy, did I knock down some quality time at Chuck E. Cheese's yesterday afternoon!"? A better option is to herd the kids to a nearby park. It's clean, it's free, it's fun, and they'll love it. If a little one accidentally spills his neon raspberry juice, it will soak into the grass. And if, God forbid, someone sustains a minor injury, let the parents sue the County. They're sure to be responsive.

- As your child opens his presents, be sure to take notes of what he receives and from whom. This can be extremely valuable information later on. For example, at his second birthday party at the local park, little Johnny might receive a toy drum set (complete with snare, cymbals, bass, etc.) from his friend Connor. You and your wife will spend months grinding your teeth, cursing the day Johnny received this "gift." When Connor's birthday finally rolls around, you will want to respond appropriately, essentially launching a salvo back at Connor's parents. In order to do so, head down to your local Toys-R-Us and look for a teenage employee who seems like he may have a clue. Slip the kid a ten-spot and ask him to show you the latest, loudest, most obnoxious toys on the market (he'll immediately know what you're looking for). The now gleeful teenage employee will give you a complete tour of the latest gadgetry. Hint: Don't settle for anything that runs on less than eight "D" batteries.

BIRTHDAY PARTIES IN THE NEW MILLENNIUM

And if those batteries can only be accessed by using a Phillips screwdriver (or better yet, a hex wrench), you've hit pay dirt. Trust us, Connor's parents will pay closer attention when buying little Johnny's gift for his third birthday!

- In spite of all of the above, don't deny your kids the birthday experience. They really do love these parties (even if they cling to your leg or cower in the corner). Aside from pre-school or family get-togethers, these are about the only times when your little ones can hang with some equally sized munchkins. Keep in mind, birthday parties are for the kids, not the parents. Suck it up (like you do when your wife asks for a back rub) and try to remember the joy on their faces as they try to blow out the candles. Let them eat cake with their fingers. Let them feel like a million bucks. Those smiles and memories are priceless and more than worth the effort.

Chapter 15

Minivan Mayhem

"In 1900, a father's horsepower meant his horses.
Today, it's the size of his minivan."
-- Unknown

No doubt about it – being a man has certain advantages. Generally speaking, most males enjoy size, strength, and speed that are superior to those of their female counterparts. We get to partake in the joys of procreation, while avoiding the physical agony of pregnancy and childbirth (yes, we suffer indirectly, but that is covered in other chapters). As we wander further and further out on thin ice, we will now stop and promptly get to the point…

Gentlemen, get ready to have your manhood tested. If it hasn't happened already, the day will come when your beloved spouse gets the brilliant idea of trading in her sporty car or SUV for that bane of parental existence – the minivan. Her argument may take a variety of forms: *convenience* ("the sliding doors are easier to get the kids in and out," or "It's easier to haul Johnny and his nine friends to the zoo in one trip"), *value* ("for what we spent on your Silverado, we could buy two Toyota Siennas!"), or even *comfort* ("you'll love the captain's chairs!"). The one thing her argument will never center upon is likely the one aspect of an automobile you value most – *style*. To date, neither of us has ever heard anyone mutter the phrase, "Honey, look at the lines on that Town & Country – it's a beauty!", or

"Have you seen that Odyssey the Schwartzes just bought? That thing looks fast just sitting in the driveway. We've *got* to get down to the Honda dealer this weekend!"

No sir. You've paid a small fortune for hideous maternity clothes. You've endured parties and baby showers that would have stopped the hearts of lesser men. You've paid premiums for cheesy baby furniture, matching décor, and reams of disposable diapers. You've spent days on your hands and knees installing safety equipment. You've single-handedly ensured your kids' pediatrician of a cozy and secure retirement. *The madness has to end!*

Have some dignity, man! Draw the line. This is the Final Frontier. Minivan? Not just *No*, but *Hell No!* Period. There can be no crack in your armor, no hesitation in your conviction, or you'll never hear the end of it. Your wife must know that discussions about minivans are as disgusting and distasteful to you as the subject of female mud wrestling is to her. It's off limits. End of discussion. Go find yourself an SUV that sits relatively low (for easy entry and exit), has a couple captain's chairs and sufficient storage capacity. And move on!

With all that said, let's assume for a moment that either:

1. The publishing of this book came too late. Without our counsel, you fell into the minivan trap, and that ugly, piece-of-crap-with-dual-sliders-on-wheels is already in your garage; or

MINIVAN MAYHEM

2. Your wife wears the pants in your family.

In either case, and assuming the minivan was purchased for your wife's convenience, make sure it becomes "her car." Let her enjoy the sliding door(s) and captain's chairs while you maintain some of your dignity by driving the "other" car. It doesn't matter the make, model, color, or condition of "your vehicle," so long as you don't have to enter the office garage in a Chrysler Town & Country or the like.

If, however, the minivan becomes your primary ride (and, therefore, schlepping the kids becomes your primary job), there are actually a few things you can do in order to lessen or minimize the impending humiliation. First, tint the windows. State laws vary in regard to which windows can be tinted and how dark the tinting can be, but generally speaking, we recommend that you tint every window, and the darker the better. And for God's sake, do your community a favor and keep the windows up and the air conditioning on. Nothing is more pathetic than seeing some jackass cruising down the road with his hairy arm hanging out the window, tapping his hand on the minivan door to the beat of the Sesame Street or Wiggles (who *are* these guys, anyway?) music in the CD player. Keep the fact that you've been neutered to yourself.

Second, be sure and keep a large trashcan in your minivan at all times. For those of you who already possess one of these boxes-on-wheels, this advice should be self-explanatory. For any of you still on the sidelines – consulting Consumer Reports for the most efficient, safest family vehicle – let us elaborate. It is absolutely unbelievable, horrifying really, how much junk can accumulate inside your kid-transporting vehicle (minivan or not) in a short period of time. Somehow, even children who are careful inside the house will toss snacks, drinks, and generally anything that is either sticky or crumbly around inside the car. It's like they're in a moving pigpen. In fact, such will be the condition of your toddler-toter that your faithful dog, who in the past was always eager to join you for the quick trip down to the hardware or sporting goods store, will now be reluctant to come along. Indeed, the dog's sole reason to enter your car now is to eat the leftovers that the kids have left behind. To this end, be sure and watch out for unusual spikes in the old fella's weight.

Third, try to maximize the distance between your children and the back of your head. Some minivans, we've noticed, have up to three or four rows of seats or benches. Stick your kid(s) in the rearmost seat, even if you're traveling with just one child. Again, the rationale here should be obvious. In driver's training, the instructor never spent any time developing in you the (now critical) skill of driving your car in a straight line with a screaming kid eighteen inches behind your right ear. In addition, by distancing yourself from Junior and his safety seat, you will minimize the chance of damaging your clothes when he decides to chuck whatever he's eating or when his raspberry juice box explodes.

MINIVAN MAYHEM

Finally, always carry your earplugs. While cruising with the kids in the minivan, you can forget about listening to your own CD's, or for that matter any music, sports, or business news. With a bare ear, you will now be condemned to listen to the senseless rantings of Barney, the Chipmunks, Elmo, and other annoying singing animals.

Relevant Testimonial #1:

> *Earlier this year, I had a uniquely horrifying experience. The event took place at an industry golf tournament. The second hole was a 165-yard par 3. I was the last in our foursome to hit and opted to use a seven iron. My tee shot appeared to be a good one, dropping in behind a big bunker which protected the front of the green.*
>
> *When the four of us walked onto the green several minutes later, my ball was nowhere in sight. We searched along the back of the green and beyond the fence which served as the out-of-bounds line. After ten minutes with no success, I finally got the bright idea to look in the hole, where I found my beloved Titleist 3. An ace—with witnesses! My glee turned to horror when my buddy pointed at the red Dodge minivan that I had apparently won. I broke into a cold sweat. All I could think of was whether or not*

the proceeds I would receive from immediately selling this piece of crap would cover the taxes due.

After five miserable minutes, we discovered that the minivan was to be awarded for a hole-in-one on the adjacent <u>fourth</u> hole (which was another par three; the vehicle had been parked on the grass area which separated the two greens). Needless to say, I was elated at this discovery and was more than happy to fork over the $828 required to buy cocktails for each of the tournament's 210 participants!

Moral of Story #1: If the Grand Prize is a minivan, don't enter the contest.

<u>**Relevant Testimonial #2**</u> :

A few years back, I was working as an engineer in the International Division of a major oil corporation. The group that I worked with was responsible for generating drilling prospects along the west coast of Africa. As part of our job duties, each of us was responsible for monitoring the drilling activity in a particular country within the region, and once a month the twelve of us would get together to give progress updates.

One such meeting was especially memorable. About half way through the one hour affair, in through the door burst one of my co-workers, a pompous Englishman named Ian. Upon his entry into the conference room, Ian seemed extremely frazzled. The older of his two boys had apparently been especially difficult en route to pre-school in Ian's minivan. As Ian's turn to present his update had passed by the time he arrived at the meeting, he was allowed to give his report immediately after I wrapped up my presentation. As I went to sit down, and as Ian passed by me on his way to the projection screen, I heard several muffled bursts of laughter from my co-workers. Upon returning to my chair, I quickly discovered the reason for their amusement.

There was Ian, waving his arms, ranting and raving about the latest happenings in western Zaire, with a partially eaten Charms Blow Pop stuck to his derrière. The thing was on there pretty good— he must have sat on it in the minivan, and his weight and warmth had pressed it firmly onto his perfectly pressed suit during his commute.

Now, if this had happened to any of the rest of us in the group, the Blow Pop in question would have been pointed out immediately. Though hilarious, the incident would have been brief. Not so with poor Ian. No one had the heart to end his unintentional comedy act, instead choosing to focus on the Blow Pop, which continued to dangle like a pendulum from his backside.

After he wrapped up his presentation, one of his fellow countrymen finally called to attention the candy in question. The ensuing tirade lasted the better part of twenty minutes and was clearly audible to people and businesses on adjacent floors. This incident, I was later informed, was one in a string of performances that eventually led to his demotion and an unwelcome, premature return to his beloved Britain.

Moral of Story #2: Keep your butt out of trouble by watching what your kids have planted on your seat.

Chapter 16

Miscellaneous Rantings and Ravings

"Having a family is like having a bowling alley installed in your brain."
-- Martin Mull

THE TOP TEN REASONS WHY AN IMPRISONED FELON IS BETTER OFF THAN THE FATHER OF A TODDLER:

10. The felon gets some *sleep*.
9. He has meals served *to* him.
8. His cell is always quiet and tidy.
7. There are no toys to trip on between his bed and the toilet.
6. He has time and space to read.
5. His chores have a beginning, an end, and a purpose.
4. He can watch whatever he wants on television.
3. His in-laws have no desire to visit or speak to him.
2. He has control over the microphone and mute button while conversing across the glass with his wife.
1. The felon gets more play.

BOGUS EXPRESSIONS:

"Sleep like a Baby"
An oxymoronic metaphor. Babies don't sleep. And when they do, you're at the office (sleeping). In the words of Leo J. Burke, "People who say they sleep like babies usually don't have them."

"EZ Asembly" (bad directions are always misspelled)
It'll take you, two neighbors, and three trips to Toys 'R Us to put the contents together.

"Childproof Cap"
At Sears, they sell pliers called "Robogrips." You may want to invest in a pair.

"Take Candy from a Baby"
Contrary to its popular use, this is an impossible task.

THINGS TO WATCH OUT FOR:

1. Your Garage and, more specifically, your tool area will become a dumping ground. Plastic jack-o-lanterns, sidewalk chalk, broken toys, (leaking) paint kits, Christmas decorations, strollers and accessories — you name it, they're piled on top of your table saw. In fact, if you ever need to get to your tools for a weekend project, you had best start looking for them on Friday

night. The key here is a swift counterattack on your part – leave a can of motor oil on the changing table or maybe a hedge trimmer in the crib. Your wife will get the point.

2. The wife will want you available at all times to discuss any and all child-related matters that occur during the workday. For this reason, it will be important for you to locate cellular "dead zones," places in your office building or around town where there is little or no cell reception. Then when she calls your mobile to inquire as to your whereabouts, you can head to the nearest dead zone, and the static and/or disconnection is not your fault.

3. Any toy inside a box which reads "Assembly Required." For items that need to be put together, most toy stores will offer assembly for $10-$20. Don't think twice. Consider this a superior investment opportunity.

4. Any resort or destination that purports to offer "family fun." To the extent that such an oxymoron actually exists, it is likely to occur at home when you get to watch the Stanley Cup in a Barcalounger while the kids play in the backyard.

5. Your wife's innate ability to track you down. In some instances, it will be as if she bribed a dentist to insert a Lo-Jack transponder into one of your fillings. For

example, don't be surprised at what happens when you stop at a friend's place on the way home from the office to grab a beer or watch a couple innings of a game. Amazingly, not minutes after your arrival, your wife will "happen" to call your buddy's wife, who will be all too happy to disclose your whereabouts.

6. Viruses. Beware the kid in Junior's playgroup with the hacking cough. Expose any member of your family to this little monster, and your whole clan will be ill by sundown. His parents have, in essence, waged germ warfare on anyone even remotely associated with the playgroup. When this happens, it is your duty to plan and execute a counterattack.

Chapter 17

A Few Closing Thoughts

"A baby is God's opinion that the world should go on."
-- Carl Sandburg

After reading our book, many of you are surely thinking that we, the authors, are raving lunatics— a couple of chauvinist pigs, both of whom should never have had children in the first place.

The truth is that both of us have wonderful lives at home, we love our wives, and we absolutely adore our kids. And though our children are still very young, we are already making some key observations and would like to pass on a few brief ideas to our readers.

First, take time to love your children, especially during the infant and toddler stages. As you sit rocking your crying baby at 4 a.m. while counting ceiling tiles, you may not always see the light at the end of the tunnel. But believe us, the joys and rewards of time spent with your child will far outweigh the difficulties, the latter of which you will tend to quickly forget. And as we're already starting to find out, their infancy and innocence are fleeting. Enjoy it while you can.

Second, your young child's ability to observe and absorb will never be greater. As a parent, you are their biggest role model, their primary focus, their idol. Conduct yourself accordingly.

Third, being a good father to your child is an enormous responsibility. It requires patience, commitment, and sacrifice. But the opportunity only happens one time per child, and you won't get a second chance. We've heard it said, and the theory is proving valid – when looking back on their lives, few older men ever regret the "extra" time they opted to spend with their family over putting in "a few more hours" at the office.

Finally, try to maintain your sense of humor. This will be challenging at times. But the ability to laugh at yourself and the predicaments you encounter will help you "survive" the first years of fatherhood and beyond.

Be grateful, and enjoy!